Student-Centered Learning by Design

STUDENT-CENTERED LEARNING BY DESIGN

Jacquelyn Whiting

Foreword by Michelle Luhtala

An Imprint of ABC-CLIO, LLC
Santa Barbara, California • Denver, Colorado

Copyright © 2021 by Jacquelyn Whiting

All rights reserved. No part of this publication may be reproduced, stored in a retrieval system, or transmitted, in any form or by any means, electronic, mechanical, photocopying, recording, or otherwise, except for the inclusion of brief quotations in a review, without prior permission in writing from the publisher.

Library of Congress Cataloging-in-Publication Data

Names: Whiting, Jacquelyn, author.
Title: Student-centered learning by design / Jacquelyn Whiting ;
   Foreword by Michelle Luhtala.
Description: Santa Barbara : Libraries Unlimited, [2021] |
   Includes bibliographical references and index.
Identifiers: LCCN 2020036783 (print) | LCCN 2020036784 (ebook) |
   ISBN 9781440877537 (paperback) | ISBN 9781440877544 (ebook)
Subjects: LCSH: Student-centered learning. | Affective education. |
   Social learning.
Classification: LCC LB1027.23 .W49 2021 (print) | LCC LB1027.23 (ebook) |
   DDC 371.39/4—dc23
LC record available at https://lccn.loc.gov/2020036783
LC ebook record available at https://lccn.loc.gov/2020036784

ISBN: 978-1-4408-7753-7 (print)
      978-1-4408-7754-4 (ebook)

25 24 23 22 21   1 2 3 4 5

This book is also available as an eBook.

Libraries Unlimited
An Imprint of ABC-CLIO, LLC

ABC-CLIO, LLC
147 Castilian Drive
Santa Barbara, California 93117
www.abc-clio.com

This book is printed on acid-free paper ∞

Manufactured in the United States of America

To Zach and Emma,
When the road doesn't rise to meet you, may you always be optimistic
and believe in your capacity to change the world.

"I know it seems like the world is falling apart but in all actuality it's a great point in your life to get a little crazy. Follow your curiosity and be ambitious with it. Don't abandon your dreams. The world needs you!"

—Larry Page, Google CEO

Contents

Foreword *by Michelle Luhtala* xi
Preface xv
Acknowledgments xxi

1—Introduction: What Is Human-Centered Design? 1
2—The Personas 7
3—A Design Process 15
4—Designing Curricula: A New Mindset for Curriculum Development 19
   How Might We Leverage Content Standards to Empower
      Informed Student Action and Civic Engagement?   *19*
5—Human-Centered Collaboration: Colleagues as Designers 35
   How Might We Enhance Student Learning through
      Transdisciplinary Colleague Collaboration?   *35*
6—Learning by Design: Putting Students at the Center as Design Thinkers 51
   How Might We Disrupt the Traditional Classroom Structure
      to Empower Students to Be Agents of Change and to
      Take Informed Action?   *51*
   Case 1: High School Sociology Class   52
   Case 2: Digital Literacy Class   58
   Case 3: Advanced Placement Chemistry   64
   Case 4: *The Great Gatsby* Essay   68
   Case 5: Ninth-Grade World History   70

Case 6: Sixth-Grade Social Studies 73
Case 7: Career and Technical Education (CTE) and Design 81
Case 8: Rethinking the Traditional Public Policy Paper in Civics Class 83
Case 9: Designing for a Multigrade Classroom 86
Case 10: Building a Safe Learning Environment in Third Grade 88
Case 11: An Entrepreneurial Educator Promoting Student Agency 90
Case 12: Solving Real-World Problems through Game-Based Design 93

7—Distance Learning by Design 99

8—Conclusions: Mindset Matters Most 107

Appendix A: Resources 111
Appendix B: Templates and Organizers 113
Appendix C: Technology Resources 121
References 123
Index 125

Foreword

As an educator with thirty years of experience, I have worked with thousands of educators in at least as many schools. I have taught in U.S. cities large and small, and in the suburbs, too. For over a decade, I have facilitated online professional development, and I teach graduate library science courses. Largely thanks to Jacquelyn Whiting's project management capacity, I coauthored a book with her, *News Literacy: The Keys to Combating Fake News* (2018, Libraries Unlimited).

There is one certainty my experience has confirmed. Teaching is hard. Between inflated class sizes, revolving administrator initiatives, parent pushback, grading student work, and now distance learning, teaching frequently feels like a grind. As much as we want to earnestly devote ourselves to tackling real problems that our learning communities face, our good intentions can get buried in the sheer overwhelmingness of our jobs.

But what if our path to exiting the daily grind lay in its very overwhelmingness? What if the very challenges that prevent us from "seeing through the trees" empowered us to find forest-scale solutions? What if we used design thinking to help us love what we do a little (or a lot, depending on your baseline) more? And what if this new thing wasn't an add-on or a time suck? What if it simplified our job instead of making it more complicated? Does that sound too good to be true? It isn't.

When Jacquelyn Whiting and I wrote *News Literacy: The Keys to Combating Fake News* during the short, but inspiring time we taught together, I was dazzled by Jackie's ability to not only solve problems, but identify them first, and then solve them. Problems, to Jackie, are opportunities for progress and change. Her approach is process oriented, which is the beauty of her mindset. This is probably why many of my current colleagues at New Canaan High School still use pedagogical strategies they learned from Jackie. She empowered teachers to scaffold learning and provide students with authentic and meaningful feedback about their learning, which resulted in better performance throughout the process—not for a better grade, but because the embedded critical thinking, reflection, and revision made the work more interesting. So it is no surprise that in this book she empowers educators to reflect on their practice and shares a replicable model that empowers students to effectively address what impedes their learning.

If you are an educator and you are wondering if this book is for you, let me assure you that it is. First of all, it is a pleasure to read. Jackie's voice rings through with all its intelligence, humor, and enthusiasm. Reading it is like having a conversation with Jackie, and for all the years I have known her, nothing gets me more jazzed about going to work tomorrow than a Jackie chat. Jackie inspires me to be my best educator self, and this book is all about that. I also want to underscore that this book is for all educators. If you teach preschool, high school, special education, or English learners—whether your school is in a city, in the country, or a remote location—this book is for you. What it prescribes does not require small class size, high test scores, or any technology whatsoever. It will show you how to empower students to check their social and emotional compass, activate their empathy, and take ownership of their own learning. Following the strategies Jackie provides will engage even the most disengaged learners. While this is the chief objective, it will engage the most disengaged teachers, too.

Jackie describes design thinking as a mindset, not a process. Modeling one of the key elements of design thinking, empathy, Jackie introduces personas and uses them to personalize the case studies she shares. This book is grounded in Jackie's extensive experience as a professional developer in education. Readers will recognize concepts from Future Design School, The Right Question Institute, and the Google Innovator Academy, just to name a few. Interdisciplinary work is featured throughout the book, and each example demonstrates the importance of designing prototypes and incorporating user feedback to improve them. Jackie provides practical, replicable strategies to engender team-wide empathy, which teach readers how to generate effective grassroots solutions to school or district-wide issues.

The design thinking mindset empowers learners to keep the problem at the heart of what they create. It encourages them to fall in love with the problem. This is important because it coaxes learners to embrace struggle and promotes divergent thinking. Through her compelling case studies, Jackie demonstrates the pedagogical value in the constraint to student-centered design to her readers.

It is unavoidable. Jackie's vision of student-centered design will improve educator practice, whether a first-year teacher or a seasoned veteran. It challenges teachers to rethink their measures of student understanding, relying instead on students' self-perception and awareness so they can chart their own path to learning success. Jackie provides strategies that will help educators qualitatively improve collaboration, and further integrate emerging and traditional literacies, and embed digital citizenship into their instruction.

Jackie highlights the social and emotional advantages to student-centered design. She demonstrates that amplifying student voice will, by default, improve school culture. Focusing on humanity as a driver for improvement may seem obvious until you reflect on what currently drives many learning communities to "improve" (e.g., test scores, promotion, dropout rates, and college acceptance). A human-centered culture helps learners adapt more agreeably to change and gives folks permission to pivot.

Your students will love you for reading this book because they will be more engaged. It challenges readers to reimagine their instructional units and assessments. With student-centered design, learners become innovators and change agents. They understand that risk is essential to learning. Through collaboration and peer-to-peer feedback, they develop trust, not only in their learning partners and teachers, but in themselves as well. This also applies to learners who avoid participating in traditional instructional settings. With this mindset, students commit to the idea and the impact of taking action.

When I finished reading the book, I immediately called Jackie to share my enthusiasm. It was fun to read, and it inspired me to improve my practice in a way that will feel easier, not harder. During the weeks that followed, I found myself returning to it, pitching it to colleagues without thinking, incorporating it into my current practice and my plans for the future. As I said in the first paragraph, Jackie inspires me to be my best educator self. Once you read this book, she will do the same for you.

—Michelle Luhtala

Preface

MY JOURNEY TO DESIGN

I invite you to explore the chapters of this book in the order they work for you depending on your role in your school and your experience with human-centered design. In fact, you may want to return to this Preface when you have finished exploring the outline of the design process and its application to teaching and learning. If you have already begun to dabble with design thinking and adopt a human-centered design mindset, you might want to begin here with my explanation of how design thinking informed the writing of this book and how I am using this mindset to define and evolve my role as innovation and technology specialist responsible for educator coaching and facilitation of professional learning.

On the Writing of This Book

My deep dive into design thinking began in the fall of 2017 when I was accepted into the Google Certified Innovator program. The application process requires that prospective attendees explain a problem in education that they wish to dedicate the next year to researching and working to solve. Prior to traveling to Stockholm, Sweden, to attend the Academy, the members of my cohort were introduced to the essential element of design thinking: empathy with your stakeholder. Through a series of exercises we each examined stakeholders in the problems we had presented in our applications and worked remotely with one another to unpack what we were learning about these people. The problem I confronted was a pervasive lack of media literacy in schools and communities. Other members of my cohort examined issues in special education, professional development, women in tech, and a host of other issues. At this time I was only a couple of months into a new job at a new school; the first exercise required me to find and interview three different people: one who was very invested in my problem and potential solutions, one who denied that my problem was solvable, and a third person somewhere in between. This was a tremendous opportunity for me to get to know some of my new colleagues and begin to understand their pedagogy. After completing these interviews, we returned to our problem and wrote a detailed explanation of why and for how long it existed, who was affected, what had been previously done about it (if anything), and why it was important to us to find a solution. We shared these exposés with another member of the cohort, and they asked five "why?" questions probing into what we had written. (More on The Five Whys in Chapter 5.)

Once at the Academy, we began the intense process of shifting from understanding design thinking as a process to adopting a design thinking mindset. Along the way, we examined our identities to understand how our strengths, challenges, fears, and experiences influenced how we understood each other. We were exposed to a myriad of tools and strategies for engaging in divergent thinking and ideation as well as feedback and prototyping. The experience was intense—at times energizing and exhilarating and other times exasperating. In sum, it was life changing. Problems—things that previously might have thwarted my interest or effort—became challenges and challenges are opportunities. Obstacles became constraints that actually liberated creative ideas never before entertained. I can't overstate how grateful I am for how participating in this program transformed my habits of mind. The Google Certified Educator program is managed by Google for Education, EdTechTeam (California, U.S.), and Future Design School (Toronto, CA). After my experience in Stockholm, I continued my study and work with Future Design School (futuredesignschool.com) for years since the Academy.

More and more I brought this mindset to the decision-making events in my personal and professional life. As my parents' health began deteriorating, my family undertook a considered examination of all of our needs and expectations for quality of life in order to develop a plan that would allow for people's needs to be met and independence maintained as much as possible. When I was assigned to teach a new course only two days before the start of school and without any historical curricular materials, this mindset allowed me to embrace the opportunity to create a student-centered learning laboratory and push the edges of my pedagogy, take risks, and fail forward. You can read about one of the design exercises the students undertook as part of our unit called "Social: The New Media" in Case 2 in Chapter 6.

The more valuable I found human-centered design to be for my life and work, the more urgently I felt a compulsion to help my students and colleagues to implement these practices in their teaching and learning as well. For a couple of years I facilitated design thinking workshops at conferences like ISTE and AASL. While such workshops are invigorating, the educators who attend those sessions are just a fraction of the educators working to transform their classrooms and libraries into student-centered learning spaces, and most of us aren't able to regularly attend such events (if at all). I am very active on professional social media and found that I was building a professional learning network (PLN) of educators from around the world who are as interested in these practices as I am, which gave rise to the opportunity to host webinars on the topic. And beyond the digital realm, I began to seek ways to connect, in person, with people where I live. To that end, I even hosted small design thinking events in my home for local educators.

I am an interdisciplinary learner by nature. As an educator I am certified as both a social studies teacher and a library media specialist. One of the many threads that connects those two educator roles is a love of reading. This is a passion that I share with many of my educator friends who are not active on social media and do not travel to conferences, and it translates into being a lifelong learner. Thus, writing a book—this book—about the power of a design thinking mindset, and including in it stories of educators whose mindset and knack for facilitating student-centered learning experiences inspire me every day, became my natural next step.

I encourage you to follow the educators whose stories are collected here, because the case studies are just small pieces of the impressive and exciting work they are doing with students in all different subjects and of all different ages. When you begin to implement what you learn from the lessons and stories in this book, please join the conversation that celebrates this work, that problem solves around obstacles, and creates new and exciting teaching and learning opportunities by using #SCLbydesign. Design is collaborative at its core; let's grow our partnership of design thinking educators committed to creating student-centered schools.

On the Defining of My Role as Innovation and Technology Specialist

On November 5, 2019, I began a new job at one of the state of Connecticut's Regional Educational Service Centers (RESCs) called Cooperative Educational Services or C.E.S. Our agency provides educational support and services to the school districts and communities in our region, including community-based education through our four school programs, as well as professional learning opportunities, strategic planning support, and other such school-district related services. My role as innovation and technology specialist is to provide progressive pedagogical support with an emphasis on innovation and meaningful use of technology for teaching and learning to the teachers in our schools and in the schools of our region. The role is part coach, part professional development design and facilitation, and, because the kind of coaching and professional learning that I provide is a new element to the menu of options at C.E.S., it is also part entrepreneurial. It is design thinking heaven!

I spent the first several weeks in my new role visiting one-on-one with the administrators and coordinators of the different programs and services the agency offers. From the special education day schools to the PreK–8 magnet school and the performing arts high school—there were so many different models of what a school can be for me to explore. I toured the schools, visited classrooms, and sat and listened while people described the best parts of their jobs, their hopes for their programs, the uniqueness of their students and those students' goals. I listened as the other PD specialists described their specialties and their work with the schools in our area. I attended the workshops they offered and the meetings of councils we host for educators from different schools to come together and network, resource share, and learn.

In between these visits I planned my own workshops. I reviewed the various sessions I hosted at conferences like AASL, ISTE, and NEASC. I examined the attendees' feedback and revised my plans and materials according to their recommendations and needs. I submitted all of the details about the session to our scheduler to be added to our calendar and distributed through her networks, and waited for people to register. And waited. And waited. And then I started to stress. What had I done wrong? Why wasn't anyone signing up? What had I missed? I had sessions on design thinking and entrepreneurship, on student voice and the power of story, on game-based learning to enhance student engagement. Aren't those important elements of pedagogy to be refined? What district isn't working on shifting their curriculum and instruction to be more student centered? What better way to accomplish that shift than through the learning available in these sessions?

One of the principles of design is giving yourself permission to pivot. Clearly, it was time for a reassessment. So I cleared a table in the middle of our workspace, spread out paper, grabbed my sharpies, and started to build a profile of the educator who I thought would attend, enjoy, and benefit from the workshops I was planning. I got to know my user (see Figure P.1).

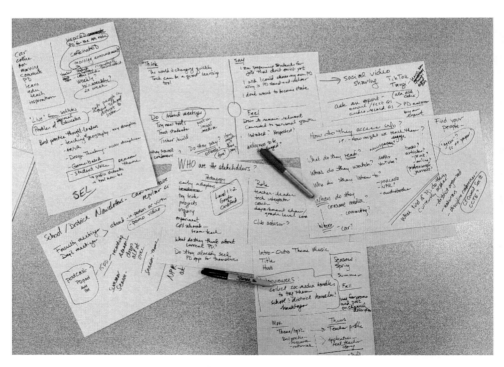

FIGURE P.1 Workshop User Profile

I started by listing what I knew about the educators who I encounter in workshops and presentations that I facilitate at large conferences like ISTE and AASL. I thought about the educators who I meet when I participate in workshops in these kinds of venues. I wondered, as educators, who are they? The list of attributes I created included roles like teacher-leader, team teacher, and club advisor. When it comes to technology, I think of them as early adopters if not innovators and certainly as the early majority on the diffusion of innovation model as depicted in Figure P.2.

Then I started to consider credentialing. My stakeholders are educators who earn microcredentials from various professional learning programs. Not just for the sake of the credential, however, they earn them as a consequence of pursuing ongoing growth in their field. They are lifelong learners—educators who are Apple Distinguished Educators and Level 2 Google Certified, as examples.

I pushed that sheet of paper aside and began a new one; this time I created an "understanding your stakeholder" matrix (see Figure 4.1, Understand Your Stakeholder), and when it came to figuring out what does my stakeholder do, this process began to accelerate. I realized that my stakeholder, the educator I was trying to reach with my sessions, does two things that all educators do:

1. Attend lots of meetings: faculty, department, grade level, 504, PPT, etc.
2. Commute to school

Boom. There it is. Two times and places where my stakeholder is a captive audience. Now, while it would be wonderful if each principal of each school in our region would invite me to introduce myself and the opportunities available at our agency to their collected faculty at a meeting, that can be a tough sell. Administrators have limited time to address their faculty and advance

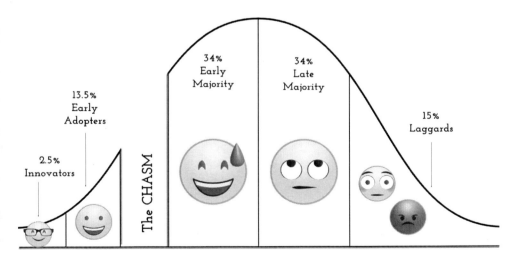

FIGURE P.2 The Theory of Diffusion of Innovation

building initiatives with everyone together in one place at the same time. While what I am offering may align with some building goals, I decided to put these meetings as a mode of access to the side and focus on the commute.

When I shared this thought process with my boss, he said, "Podcast!" To which I responded, "Yes, and, NPR." (More on "Yes! And . . ." in Chapters 5 and 6.) Just down the road from our building are the offices of our regional NPR station. Wouldn't it be excellent, I wondered out loud, if that station included the work of our agency in some of their coverage of local events. Imagine if, in one of their broadcast programs, they did a story on lifelong learning and included how we nurture growth mindset, forward failure, and professional development in the educators of our area. And, when we collaborate with community organizations, like the local zoo, to host "staycation" events for educators and their children that embed professional learning for educators to take back to the classrooms, how great would it be if local NPR did a story on that?

And, yes, of course, we need a podcast. We need to create some media, easily consumable while driving, that examines and unpacks issues in education and progressive, research-based pedagogy and profiles educators in our region tackling those issues and implementing best practices. Listeners can learn from what they hear on the podcast—in our early stages we are calling it "Morning Announcements" as in PD for your AM drive to work—and if they find certain content particularly meaningful, they can join us for a workshop to explore the practice hands-on and prepare to implement it in their teaching.

So my new role has become to push at the boundaries of what is being done and what has always been done. My focus is to help our agency not just stay relevant as the Fourth Industrial Revolution and the gig economy rapidly evolve the needs and opportunities of the world into which our students graduate, but lead. Leading learning. Leading in being comfortable living in the discomfort of change. What better place for a design thinking, lifelong learner and educator to land?

Acknowledgments

I owe a tremendous debt of gratitude to the educators who gave their stories to this book and shared their expertise with me as colleagues, friends, and members of my professional learning network.

Of my most recent colleagues: Meredith Ramsey when brand new to teaching, engaged me in design conversations around her unit planning, and opened her classroom to me as a coteacher. I am inspired by her grit, enthusiasm, commitment to all of her students, and passion for history. Michelle Maher, another social studies teacher, was among the first among her peers to trust me and what appeared to be my unorthodox methods during a curriculum writing workshop. We bonded and embarked on the design sprint and sociology project described here. And Drew Colati who was my thought-partner and critical friend for so many student-centered classroom adventures and for designing and facilitating multiple professional development experiences.

When writing about her work with design, I could barely scratch the surface of the incredible talents of Ashley O'Connor. In addition to the DIY course that is described here, she teaches web design, game design, and other courses all with a design mindset. She has also published a children's book about technology, which is infused with project ideas to nurture children's creativity.

Look no further than my relationships with Arianna Lambert, Rachel Swanson, and Jen De Lisi-Hall to understand the power of a digital professional learning network. While our opportunities to see each other face-to-face are rare, indeed—maybe once a year if we are lucky—these three educators are among the most creative, generous, forward thinking, and inspiring people I know. Any time I send a question or idea, they are quick to "Yes, and . . ." respond. In their own ways, each has served as a mentor, role model, and critical friend for which I am very grateful.

Not only do I call Michelle Luhtala my mentor, she is also a colleague and friend. My growth as a librarian, specifically, and an educator more generally is a result of her critical friendship. The uncanny parallel elements of our lives just serve to secure our bond. I am so grateful that she lent her wisdom and experience to the Foreword for this book.

Special thanks to my editors and mentors at Libraries Unlimited and School Library Connection: Sharon Coatney, Jane Cullina, David Paige, and Emma Bailey. Gratitude also to Future Design School and Google for Education whose collaboration resulted in the Certified Google Innovator program that put me on this professional learning path. The influence of these people and organizations has steered my creative pursuits in ways I could never have anticipated.

Of all the people who contributed to the writing of this book, I am most indebted to my life partner, Brett Baker. When imposter syndrome gets the better of me and I begin to succumb to self-doubt, Brett warns me—with a smile and a hug—that I better not assert a growth mindset ever again if I don't rally and recommit. He is my best editor, my champion, my challenger, my ally, and my heart.

1

Introduction: What Is Human-Centered Design?

It is so much fun to build something. I am energized when I am trying to solve a problem, or address a shortcoming, when I am creating something that interests and intrigues me. Maybe I am building a curated wardrobe for a new job or renovating an outdated and poorly functioning bathroom in my house or planning an excursion for an upcoming break from school. In each instance, I am the designer, and I am a primary—if not sole—beneficiary of what is being planned.

Human-centered design challenges me to shift my mindset and focus it on other people. Consider the wardrobe: how and from what materials would each item be constructed, and why would I select and pair them? And how might the whole ensemble be curated differently if the assembled clothing was to be shared with someone else, even someone else in the same job? For example, I certainly struggle to endure in high heels for a whole day while someone else may feel heels are necessary to provide physical presence in power meetings. When it comes to those bathroom renovations, we must accommodate the needs that all members of the family have for the bathroom in order for it to be universally functional. I may not need a seat in the shower, while my elderly parents who live with us might. And, would my vacation be more fun if someone else came along? What are their preferences and what travel accommodations might they need? Perhaps different food or sleep needs must be accounted for in order to maximize our mutual enjoyment of the trip.

Unless I engage each of these stakeholders in deep conversations about how their clothing, or bathroom, or upcoming break from work has an impact on the quality of their day-to-day lives, I am excluding them or making assumptions about them. When planning these events or designing these products, the needs, concerns, hopes, and aspirations of the stakeholders must be at the center of the process. Maybe when it comes to planning a vacation or a home renovation, this is how we go about making and executing plans. I wonder, when we write curriculum, plan units, and implement lessons, who are the stakeholders? Certainly we, the educators who will implement the curricular plan, have a vested interest in its scope and sequence. So, too, perhaps do the members of the board of education who sanction its implementation. And the students, whose ability and willingness to engage in the learning experiences, whose progress will be monitored and evaluated, are significant stakeholders as well. Which prompts me to wonder: where are each of these people considered, accounted for, and represented in the design process?

In a nutshell, human-centered design is a creative process, and once you have lived it enough, it becomes a mindset that takes into account—at every stage of development—the needs of the people most affected by what is being constructed. To understand the problem I am trying to solve, I must examine the needs of the people who live with the problem and will live with the solution. I am not designing for them as much as I am designing with them. I must empathize with them, understand what they think and believe and why they do what they do, then how I proceed keeps them at the center of the process, enables me to leverage their motivations, and means the designed solution will improve their experiences, productivity, satisfaction, and overall quality of life.

This might seem basic and intuitive. And with the right mindset, it is. It is the process used by architects designing structures to serve the needs of the people who will live and work within them, by graphic designers creating media to deliver information to the public, by product engineers planning the features in a new model of product being readied for the consumer market. When these things are done well, we don't want them, we need them. We buy them and use them because they improve the quality of our lives.

Schools and districts are undertaking social-emotional learning initiatives and adopting SEL programs. While SEL includes more than just empathy, the importance of empathy to human-centered design makes it a valuable, authentic means of seamlessly integrating important elements of SEL into our established curricula. Like argumentative writing, or figure drawing, or critical reading, empathy is a skill that requires coaching and practice. If it is reduced to a vocabulary word—simply a term that students learn to define, rather than a muscle they strengthen through exercise—then authentic connections cannot be built, insights will always be limited, and solutions to societal problems will be incomplete at best. Students must have intentional opportunities to shift their attention to the needs, interests, and experiences of another person—to make space in their psyche for accepting someone else's story. I often told my students that once you know something you cannot unknow it, and your worldview will permanently change. Our goal, as educators, is to expand that view, and consistent practice walking in the shoes of other people is essential to that growth.

In the Netflix documentary series *Abstract: The Art of Design* (bit.ly/AbstractNetDoc), each episode focuses on the design work of someone at the forefront of their field. Every one of the designers profiled in the first two seasons speaks about the importance of empathy to their work. Each episode has pushed me to think and rethink how I see school, libraries, classrooms, authentic collaboration, and assessment. Whether it is the ergonomics of the driver's seat in my car, an album cover from my childhood, or the products in my mother's toy store, even the typeface used in this book, engaging with this documentary series has prompted me to reconsider all aspects of my environment—of the built world—and how they are the product of the imagination and collaboration of teams of designers, all working with their stakeholders in mind. I highly recommend watching it.

Educators *are* designers. Working within the institutional constraints of our schools and districts, we design classrooms, libraries, and other learning spaces. We design curricula, instructional materials, and assessments. We design field trips, open houses, parent conferences, communication platforms, and more. When we design with the students, colleagues, and families who will use and experience these things at the center of an iterative process, we are using a design thinking mindset. And, of course, we do have these groups somewhere in mind; this book and the cases studies examined in it, are a reminder to take the time to understand those stakeholders in nuanced ways and keep them in the front of our minds when we design. We can't avoid the constraints within which we do this work—our curricular standards, our budgets, and time are just a few of those constraints. We can reframe our perception of these constraints and of the problems we face. When we see them not as obstacles to meeting our obligations and instead as opportunities to innovate our system, we have reframed our mindset. We are able to leverage our insights about our stakeholders to liberate creative ideas that are possible despite the boundaries. In Chapter 6 you will read the stories of educators from across North America who embrace a human-centered design mindset and see how when they confront the challenges that they face in their classrooms and schools from an optimistic perspective with a belief in their and their students' ability to affect positive change in their classrooms and communities, incredible ideas surface and potent solutions result.

In order to keep stakeholders at the center of our learning process, this book revolves around several personas. They include students, classroom teachers, other faculty members, and families. Their needs inform the models and case studies presented in Chapter 6 where real examples of design applied to the classroom are explored and teachers who have a design thinking mindset and teach their students to think like designers share their stories. This book is written with those personas in mind. I hope you identify with some of them; I hope you recognize in them concerns, beliefs, fears, hopes, and interests that members of your learning community share. Let these personas help you get to know your students, their families, and your colleagues in a nuanced way so as to inform your design. Consider what questions you need to ask to get to know them better. How can you hear what they say and see what they do in a new way? Furthermore, the case studies are all the real stories of real practicing educators. They have all agreed to share their story so that we can learn from each other. I encourage you to follow them on social media and continue learning from and with them.

So much is being written about design thinking that I share Michael Cohen's (@TheTechRabbi) concern that it will become another buzzword that starts to be ignored. Nothing has so transformed my pedagogy and educational practice as design thinking. It is a mindset rooted in optimism. It is a protocol that is iterative and requires empathy. Throughout this book I will unpack the wisdom of master educators and practitioners on the forefront of design and share examples of design thinking applied to curriculum, collaboration, and student-centered learning that you can adopt, adapt, and use in your school, your library, your classroom with your students and colleagues. And I invite you to share your plans, successes, shortcomings, and ideas so that we can continue to expand our capacity for creative problem solving and contribute our insights and points of view to each other's work. Please use #SCLbydesign and tag me—@MsJWhiting on Twitter and @jacqueylnwhiting on Instagram. I am looking forward to the conversation!

Notes

Recognizing that one size doesn't fit all (or even most), the students created multiple pathways through their argument just as they charted multiple pathways through their learning. Which serves to me as evidence that they are thriving in this learning environment.

2

The Personas

What follows in this section is a collection of character profiles. None of these people are real. I have created them to embody and reflect the experiences, attitudes, and beliefs of students and educators, in general, without any intentional depiction of a particular person. They may remind you of people you know. They may challenge you to think in new ways about members of your learning community. Ultimately, you may, when you embark on design endeavors, use these personas as models for gaining insight into the people with and for whom you are designing.

CLASSROOM TEACHERS

Cheryl

Midcareer Teacher

I want my students to care about what they are learning. I like trying new projects, and I am not afraid to learn new technology and see how it can help my students be creative. It is hard to make time for lots of new stuff with all the content I have to cover and the grade pressure that students feel. I mean we talk about taking risks, but they don't want to fail—or falter—and I don't want to waste their time or my time if we aren't going to get something out of a new experience. There is so much that is important for them to learn and learn to do, and we just can't do it all.

Add to that the budget cuts we keep facing. The cracks are starting to appear as our classes get bigger, our team-taught programs are cut, and we have fewer support personnel in our classes with students who need extra support. Cocurricular activities are disappearing. Students were already paying to play, and now they pay for clubs, too. Who wants to take risks when the administrators are deciding which staff to cut?

Julie

Veteran Teacher

I've been teaching for a long time—twenty-four years! I know that all this new technology and all these young teachers have changed my profession. But, I just don't have the ability to keep up with it all. That's OK. I know that good teaching is all based on strong relationships with my students, and that is something that I know how to do really well. In terms of collaborating with my colleagues—I remember when we used to be a small school and we did things together. We would get together for coffee once a month just to share ideas and articles that we had read—it was really enriching! Now that we have grown to be a bigger school, we have become isolated, and people are too busy to meet like we used to do. Besides, all the young teachers just want to use fancy technology and call it collaboration. I think that all our social media has actually made us worse at working together, not better! Real collaboration has to happen face-to-face. And people wonder why students are so stressed out.

Darren

New Teacher

This is my third year teaching. I don't think I have ever been this tired. I am lucky to have a couple of colleagues in my department who have taken me under their wings, so to speak, and are really valuable mentors. A couple of others see me as "a tech-obsessed millennial." There is so much to this job, and I knew from my university program I would have to make data-informed decisions, and that formative assessment was really important. Now that I'm doing it, I realize how much it is to manage and really understand for it to be meaningful. Plus the IEPs and 504s and data privacy, not to mention learning the names and faces of my students and my new colleagues and keeping their parents in the loop. Oh, and, of course, there is keeping up with the content so the students trust my knowledge. And the grading. Who knew? Now we are approaching another election and I'm teaching civics. Wow, discussions can get tense. At least on this point my colleagues agree. We are walking on eggshells when it comes to navigating the current political climate in the classroom. And this isn't just about any particular election. So many topics—privilege, bias, gender, feminism, the climate crisis—feel off-limits. But should they be?

Kai

New to This School, Not to the Profession

I have been teaching for eleven years, and when my family relocated across the state last year, I was excited to join this faculty. By reputation, it is a good school in a high-achieving community. I was hoping that I would be able to collaborate with my colleagues in different subject areas, but there isn't a culture of collaboration here. On top of that, I used to teach in an urban district. The community was diverse. So was the student body and, to some extent, the faculty. I think I am experiencing a little culture shock at my new school. Some people treat me as a token—others "don't see my color" as they like to say. As a new person in the school, I don't really know if I can rock the boat very much. At the same time, there is a lot of room for this community to expand its cultural empathy and awareness. I feel isolated and tired, which I don't like. While there are perks to teaching at a school with bells and whistles, I'm not sure if the trade-off is worth it to me.

OTHER FACULTY MEMBERS

Mitch

School Counselor

There are so many pressures on students today—from their families and teachers. From colleges. Not to mention from peers and social media. Increasingly, I feel like my students' only ally to diffuse pressure and build self-efficacy, which I am trying to do while also building schedules, tracking graduation requirements, managing 504s, prepping college applications, fielding parent phone calls, and all of the other tasks of my day.

I want teachers to be my partner—aren't we all supposed to want what is best for the students? Sometimes teachers are the biggest obstacle to helping a kid.

Teachers just don't understand that we know a lot about students and families that you don't. You need to trust us more and not ask so many questions about what you can't know. We are supposed to be a team.

Lois

Library Learning Commons

I manage a large budget in order to maximize print, digital, and hardware resources for the whole school. I analyze, weed, and supplement our print and electronic collection constantly while maintaining a flexible learning commons space and supervising 150 students during study hall. For some students my space is a real refuge. Unless you have worked in a library you have no idea how much goes into database maintenance, collection development, etc. Most people don't realize I have my own curriculum and learning standards to implement. Call it research or call it inquiry, it just isn't sexy, so I feel overlooked unless there is some sort of maker project involved. I strive to stay at the front of the digital learning curve, but my school doesn't make time for that kind of literacy and self-regulation. People seem to think that librarians are irrelevant since anything they need to know they can find online. As a result, elementary and middle school teacher librarians are being cut from schools across my state. If it weren't for accreditation mandates, more high school librarians would be cut, too.

Gloria

Building Administrator

This is my fourth year as one of the assistant principals at my school. I still remember the excitement and pressures of the classroom (unlike some of my administrative colleagues). When I do an observation, sometimes I miss teaching, though I am getting into a routine with the responsibilities of my position.

I have to admit, I am surprised by how much of my time is spent on discipline issues and parent complaints and concerns instead of implementing vision and building progressive culture. Sometimes I wonder, where are the passions and needs of the students in all of this?

Before becoming an assistant principal, I taught at this school, and teachers who used to be my friends now see me as having gone to the dark side. I think we have a morale problem among the faculty. And, if it hasn't already, that will filter to the students, too.

Stanley

Athletic Director

A lot of important learning can and should happen in health and PE and on the athletic fields. More than any other department, we are uniquely positioned to really invest in the education of the whole person. Cocurricular challenges and experiences matter. My coaches support teachers by reinforcing the importance of the classroom from behavior to learning and grades. I wish the same respect that is conferred on a core academic teacher was afforded to my health and PE faculty.

I feel like there is a wall between me and the teaching faculty. I don't think it is all in my head that by some people I am seen as the outsider, not really administration, until (of course) a student exercises poor behavior judgment and suddenly they are an athlete behaving poorly and I am taken to task. We do what we can to prevent fans from becoming fanatics; we do take sportsmanship seriously, so sometimes I am horrified by things I hear them chant in the stands. We really are trying to address it, and it is a wider national cultural problem, not just our school or district.

SECONDARY STUDENTS

Benjamin

Content with Average

I can think of a lot of places I would rather be all day than school. Well, places that would be better if I could go there with my friends. Once we all get home we hang out in our video games. I mean, I'm never absent, I do varsity sports,

I don't skip classes. My mom would make my life hell if I did. But I don't like school. I do like some of my teachers—like Mr. C. who I have for history. He is funny and sarcastic and gets my sense of humor. I don't like history, but I don't mind going to his class because I like him. I also like band. The band teacher is one of the most popular teachers in the school. The rest of my teachers are *meh*. I like my coach. We all like Coach. He gets pies for us on the last day of the season, and on game days we dress like him. I don't do homework. What's the point? It's a waste of time. I know I can do it, the teachers know I can do it so . . . why do it? I can get A's in some of my classes (mostly electives) with a little work. And B's in others. I get some C's with no effort and I'm good with that. I really just want to be left alone. As the number of kids in my classes goes up, it is easier to avoid too much teacher attention.

Naomi

Presentation vs. Reality

I am a two-season varsity athlete—have been since my freshman year. Off-season I play in a club league. Next year I will be captain. I take three AP classes this year, and next year I will take two more. I never miss school. I like most of my teachers, and I think they like me, too. I haven't read a book simply for interest or fun since middle school; back then I loved to read. Now I do a minimum of 4 hours of homework every night—more on the weekends—so who has time for fun? I also try to see my dad for a visit on the weekends since I live full time with my mom. When I can fit it in around school and my part-time job, I take metalsmithing classes because, other than my sport, that is one of my passions. And I try to volunteer because it matters and because of college. I'm already behind deciding where to go after I graduate. Last night, I collapsed on my kitchen floor in a fit of crying. I couldn't explain why, and all it did was mean I was that much later starting on my work.

Adrian

Budding Activist

This year at school, I tried to start a Gay-Straight Alliance (GSA) for students in my school, but the administration said that I wasn't allowed to unless we got parents to sign a release form. It's completely unfair—students don't need to get a release form to join the art club or the debate team. Those students are even celebrated all over the school's social media.

This all started last year when we held an event and were asked to take down any rainbow decorations because "rainbows are associated with Pride." Instead, we sold cupcakes with rainbow-dyed batter and raised $200 for charity. The school then would not allow us to donate the money to a LGBTQ organization. Research shows the existence of GSA programs has diminished the amount of harassment directed toward LGBTQ students. This is everyone's fight, not just for those in the LGBTQ community. This is about justice, and this should be something that we all care about. We should all want to fight for the rights of the students in the community.

PRIMARY/MIDDLE SCHOOL STUDENTS

Jay

Sixth Grader

I didn't want to start school this year. My dad is in the army, and he's not home right now. My brother, sister, and I get to talk to him on the phone or Facetime with him with my mom, too, on her phone. It's not the same as having him at home.

My mom works while we are at school during the day and my Nana and Pop come over to our house a lot. Nana is a good cook. She makes the best meatballs! And Pop likes when I read to him from my books.

I play baseball. My dad is the coach for my team, but he couldn't do it last spring. Maybe for the next season, he said. Pop watched the world series with me. My team didn't make it, but Pop said it was fun to watch anyway. He throws the ball with me in the yard and comes to all my games to cheer for me and my team.

My birthday is next week. Mom is taking me to Dave and Busters with my friends, and we are going to have pizza and cake there. She said she will take pictures to send to dad, because he likes to know what we are all up to while he has to be away. She always tries to do fun things with us. She said that this isn't the first time dad had to go away for the army, and she and my dad think this might be the last time. We both hope so, and we are proud of him for serving. When he gets home, I hope he can come to my school and talk to my class about the army. We always have someone do that for Veterans Day.

Antonella

Fifth Grader

I was born in Guatemala. My moms adopted me when I was just a baby. I love school. This year, I have the best teacher. Every day she tells me how happy she is to see me. She knows that I am smart, so she gives me special challenges to help me learn more.

My moms say that I am artsy because I am good at drawing and I love to dance. They make movies of me dancing with my friends and with my dog, Quetzal (she is named after the town where I was born) and post them on Instagram.

On "Special Friends" day in my class both of my moms came to class. My friends ran up and gave them both hugs. Some people asked questions about them. My teacher said that family is who loves you, which is true because my friend Emi's special friend was her Grammy.

Jocelyn

Third Grader

I just finished reading *Flora and Ulysses*. Next I'm going to read *Freckle Juice* because my friend Julia said it was really good. For my birthday I asked for lots of books so I can read them in the car when we go on trips. It's almost ski season, which means we will be in the car a lot on the weekends.

Sometimes my mom and dad will let us watch movies on the iPad, but we have a limit. When the timer goes off, screens have to go away. Sometimes I'm playing a game and I don't want to turn it off. But I do. When I go to my friend Sam's house, there are no time limits, so we can play as long as we want to. Her older sister and her friend make lots of TikTok videos. My brother is in her grade and said that Sam's sister has lots of followers. My mom said that Sam's sister would get better grades if she spent less time making videos and more time doing her schoolwork. I like getting good grades and always do the work my teacher tells me to do.

Notes

These are life skills....
Every day we fight against our students'
fear of trying.

3

A Design Process

While design thinking is a mindset, design is an iterative process. Consult the people and organizations at the forefront of this field (there is a list of whom to follow at the end of this book), and you will find illustrations and explanations of the model they employ. With slight variations in wording, they are all very similar, so I encourage you to adopt the framework or illustration that pleases you. Each will guide you down an iterative (or, if you prefer computational language, recursive) path that begins with empathy.

Successful execution of a design process requires you to:

1. abandon linear patterns, and
2. think in possibilities.

Which is to say beyond what you already know and do and toward untried measures and strategies. Also, the process requires you to suspend judgment: of the problem, of the stakeholders, of the ideas being brainstormed, of the feedback you receive. Design is the ultimate inquiry process, and for inquiry to be complete, satisfying, and productive, it must be thorough in the consideration of possibilities and points of view.

Design is a team process. A lone designer too easily falls into his/her/their familiar patterns and ways of seeing the world. Ironically, most librarians work in isolation as the only certified LMS in their school. Most teachers work in isolation from other teachers in their school when they are the only teacher in their classroom. I encourage you to read this book with a team—either an in-person group in your learning community or as part of the #SCLbydesign community. Practice and implement the exercises in this book with your collaboration team. Design is NOT parallel play. You aren't going to be sitting side by side each doing all the work by yourself. You will be collaborating: combining your unique talents, experiences, and points of view, which helps you overcome shortcomings and obstacles. Out of collaboration is borne a product that no one designer could create alone. The more diverse the team, the deeper the insight you can gain into the needs of your stakeholders, the more wild and potential-laden your ideation will be, and the more profound the impact of work will be.

On the next page is my map of the design process (Figure 3.1). In each section of this book I will refer to and elaborate on each stage. While arrows direct your eye from one stage to the next stage, in application you may loop back to previous stages to seek deeper insight and reconsider possibilities. For each example that I explore, I will refer to one or more of the personas as the stakeholders in the design. The work being done will be with them in mind, to satisfy a need they have individually or as a member of their learning community. I trust that you will recognize many of the personas, colleagues, and students at your school. I hope that the examination of those personas in this book helps you to see untapped potential in them that you can leverage to create student-centered learning experiences at your school. Let's get started!

FIGURE 3.1 Design Process

Notes

Throughout the process, students' thinking was visible, which made it easier for me and for the students to evaluate the work that was being done.

4

Designing Curricula: A New Mindset for Curriculum Development

How Might We Leverage Content Standards to Empower Informed Student Action and Civic Engagement?

Cheryl, Julie, Darren, and Kai. Those are our teacher personas. Have you written curricula before with a team like them? Can you imagine being on a curriculum team with them? I hope so! Perhaps they are coming to this collaborative curriculum team aspirational with the best intentions for a comprehensive curriculum that adheres to requisite standards. Maybe they are driven by a hope that this time, the curriculum created will match their pedagogy and beliefs about good teaching practices and content interest areas. While we consider the members of the curriculum writing team, also keep in mind the students—the ones who will be learning via the curriculum outline; they are Zach, Emma, and Adrian at the secondary level or Jay, Antonella, and Jocelyn at the primary level. How might the curriculum be designed to reflect their interests, skills, community, and needs?

STEP 1 IN OUR DESIGN PROCESS IS TO IDENTIFY A PROBLEM OR GOAL

Our goal is to develop a new curriculum guide. Step 1: Check! When curriculum is being written, or rewritten, usually it is because there is an opportunity to fill a niche or update how a school approaches student skill development and content mastery. Maybe a new course has been approved in your school or new standards have been released for your discipline or a new standardized assessment is being introduced at your grade level. Either way, a somewhat external factor has forced your team to reconsider what you do, how you do it, and what you ask students to do.

As part of curriculum writing teams over the last three decades, I have seen two possible outcomes to the well-intentioned and focused work of these teams: creating something that looks and feels a lot like what we already have and do (staying in our comfort zone) or shifting how we think about our students' processes of learning and demonstrations of learning, which results in something new, untried, and either exciting or scary depending on the mindset of the teacher who receives the curriculum and is charged with implementing it. Granted, there is a middle ground between these outcomes. Maybe the new curriculum is comprised of three familiar, rehashed units from pre-existing documents and one new, "out-there" unit. Maybe the team consciously chose to write only one risky unit, because they thought about the teachers who would be implementing it and decided any more than that one unit would be too hard to sell. That unit alone might be asking a lot. I think you get the idea: writing curriculum is an opportunity to reexamine what we do and why we do it. It is an opportunity to stop and reflect on who our students are as learners, today, which differs from the students we had five years ago, ten years ago, and certainly differs from whom we were as students back in our primary and secondary years. It also requires us to confront ourselves and ask of ourselves and each other, what are the limitations in our point of view when it comes to this process? Like Julie, are we invested in connectedness yet reticent to see and use technology for collaboration? Or are we like Darren, comfortable with technology but worried more about the political maelstrom incited by some of the content. Or perhaps we come to the team like Kai, experienced, with lots of ideas, yet feeling like an outsider on multiple levels. We design as a team so each of us can push other people past their comfort zone while allowing ourselves to be pushed out of ours.

STEP 2 IS TO DEVELOP EMPATHY WITH THE STAKEHOLDERS IN OUR PROCESS

The students are significant stakeholders in our work. Yes, the teachers, administrators, parents, and boards of education are as well. Students outnumber them all. Students are the direct recipient of the learning experiences our new curriculum enables. So, who are they? What do they think and feel about school? What do they say about the processes and content of their learning? What do they do—both at school and in their free time? Choose one of the student personas to examine, and use the "brain" organizer on the next page to guide you in unpacking who this student is as a stakeholder in the curriculum we are going to write. You will find a blank organizer that you can reproduce and use with your design teams (bit.ly/SHorganizer) as well as the completed one that can serve as a model (see Figures 4.1 and 4.2).

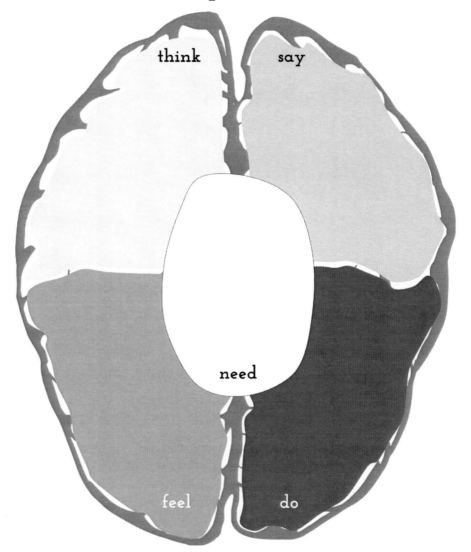

FIGURE 4.1 Understand Your Stakeholder

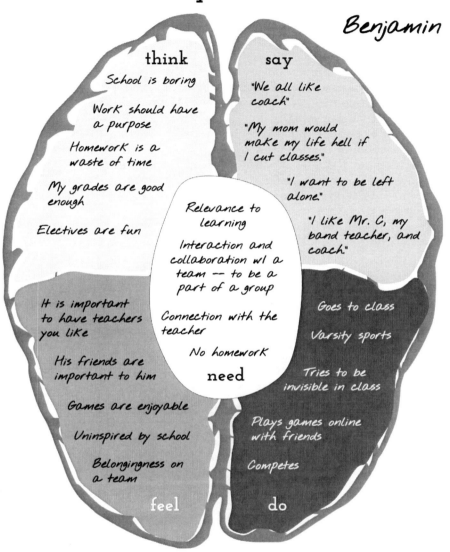

FIGURE 4.2 Student (Benjamin) Completed

Now, with all the prognostication about the unknown jobs of the future and the rapidly changing skill sets necessary for that future, we might then keep in mind that we are writing curriculum to be delivered to students whose skill sets and needs will be evolving in ways that we can't necessarily predict. The curriculum must evolve just as the students must develop habits of mind that include flexible thinking, adaptability, comfort with ambiguity, intellectual curiosity, and creativity.

Are you starting to see a problem? Moore's law has come to education. Gordon Moore (cofounder of Fairchild Semiconductor and CEO of Intel) made a prescient observation in 1965. In a nutshell, Moore said that the capacity of integrated circuits was going to double every year. Which means the computing power doubles every year while the cost goes down. Whether you were in elementary school in the era of the dial-up modems or the era of the iPhone, you have witnessed this exponential change. In education this means that the acquisition, processing, and conveying of information is changing at an exponential rate. And we are trying to write curricula that have relevance and staying power. This is a blessing and a curse.

OK. So we have a problem. It's messy, unpredictable, and complicated. And if you walk around inside it for a while it's also exciting and provocative. Can you see that? Can you feel the potential inherent in the challenge? We are going to write curricula to satisfy standards and tests we didn't create to be delivered to students whose world is changing so rapidly we can't predict their abilities and needs. At Future Design School (futuredesignschool.com and @fdesignschool) they have a mantra for this step in the design process: "Fall in love with the problem, not the solution." That's what we are going to do now.

STEP 3 IS TO MAKE INTERPRETATIONS ABOUT YOUR STAKEHOLDERS AND YOUR PROBLEM BASED ON THE INSIGHTS YOU GAINED FROM YOUR STAKEHOLDERS

What assets have you identified? What concerns do you have? What surprises did you encounter? When you consider all of this information, you can build a problem statement and then build the key to problem solving: your "How might we . . ." question.

If you are using this text to guide you through your curriculum writing process, you need to identify the constraints within which you will be designing. Usually, we think of constraints as limiting and reductive of what we could do without them. Let's shift that mindset. Constraints are what will prompt us to think beyond our go-to measures and find wild, outlandish ideas that just might be the key to our new curriculum being a vibrant, relevant, and living document. So what is a constraint? To start, standards are constraints. So is the length of the school year or the duration of a course. So is the budget. On the next page is a template (bit.ly/ProbAssetQ) that you can reproduce and use to guide your team through the interpretation phase: identifying and describing your problem, incorporating your assets and insights, and the first draft of your "How might we . . ." question. As with the previous organizer, there is also a completed version of the template to serve as a model for you (see Figures 4.3 and 4.4).

Problem Statement

(<u>stakeholder</u>) needs (<u>unmet need</u>) because (<u>insight/asset</u>).

_____ needs _____ because _____
(stakeholder)

_____

Resources & Insights

_____ *likes…*
(stakeholder)

_____ *knows s/he/they is good at…*
(stakeholder)

_____ *wishes…*
(stakeholder)

Build a Draft Question

How might we _____ in order to _____ ?

How might we… ?

How might we… ?

How might we… ?

FIGURE 4.3 Problem Template

Problem Statement
(stakeholder) needs (unmet need) because (insight/asset).

Benjamin needs interactive and collaborative classroom experiences because those are the key attributes to the activities in which he is most engaged.

Resources & Insights
Benjamin likes… online video games with his friends, his team and his coach, competition, teachers who get him, electives (the courses he chooses).

Benjamin knows he is good at… sports, teamwork, getting by

Benjamin wishes… he didn't have homework, he had more choice at school

Build a Draft Question
How might we _____ in order to _____ ?

How might we enhance our curriculum with game-based learning experiences?

How might we engage students in real-world problem solving so they see the relevance of their learning to their lives?

How might we enhance our use of collaboration so that students work in class teams with the same commitment they give to their clubs, sports, theater, jobs and other co- and extracurricular engagements?

FIGURE 4.4 Problem Template Completed

You might already have noticed that Chapters 4, 5, and 6 of this book are introduced by a question that begins with the phrase "How might we . . ." and I think it is important to examine the construction of that question stem. "How" is inherently a problem-solving orientation—it puts us in a solution-seeking frame of mind. "Might" is mighty. Please don't use the word "can" in its place. Might has an important impact on our solution-seeking frame of mind. It opens our thinking to possibilities, not current realities. "Can" asks us to consider what we already know how to do. "Might" helps our thinking diverge to a range of ideas that are unexplored and ripe for innovation. And "we." Design, as we have discussed, is a collaborative process. No one person is responsible or able to do this alone. Parts of the process (as we will see with brainstorming in the ideation phase) are about divergent thinking, so the more diverse the team the better. Others are about convergent thinking so the team has to hash out ideas to reach agreement. It is the combining, rehashing, recombining of insights, talents, experiences, and ideas of the team members that results in a solution that exceeds what any individual team member could accomplish alone. How. Might. We.

At this point, you have a few drafts of HMW questions. Now we are going to refine them by considering how the needs of our stakeholders and our constraints intersect. For this step, there is another reproducible template for you to use with your design team (bit.ly/HMWCopy) as well as a completed version to serve as a model (see Figure 4.5). Between those two illustrations you will find a list called "The Fourth Word" (see Figure 4.6). We've already unpacked how, might, and we. Next is the fourth word, and your choice of verb for the fourth slot will unleash your assets and insights to overcome your constraint (see Figure 4.7).

How might we _____ (the 4th word)

to help _____ (insight, resource, motivation, etc.)

_____ (describe the stakeholder)

who need _____ (unmet need)

to _____ (goal)

FIGURE 4.5 HMW Template

How might we ... (the 4th word)

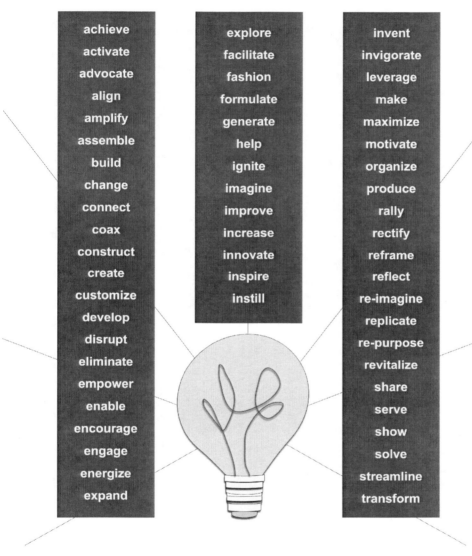

FIGURE 4.6 The Fourth Word

How might we transform _____
(the 4th word)

our new curricula _____
(insight, resource, motivation, etc.)

to help digital age students _____
(describe the stakeholder)

who need Interactive, real-world experiences _____
(unmet need)

to demonstrate mastery of the _____ standards?
(goal)

FIGURE 4.7 HMW Model

On the model you can fill in the last blank with whichever standards you are addressing. Whether you are applying a dimension of the inquiry arc from the C3 national social studies standards, the Next Gen science standards, the AASL standards, Common Core . . . you name it.

> How might we transform our new curricula to help digital age students who need interactive, real-world experiences to demonstrate mastery of the AASL Curation standard?

Notice that the HMW question now includes our goal (new curricula), our assets and insights (digital age, interactive, real-world) and our constraint (the standards). With a little reframing of our mindset and a different fourth word we could use the standards as an asset. Try this version of the HMW question on for size:

> How might we leverage the AASL Foundation: Curation to help digital age students who need interactive and real-world experiences to become engaged in their communities and take informed action?

These questions were derived from an examination of one of the student personas. Consider how the questions might differ if the assets and insights that inform its development were derived from one (or more) of the other student personas? How might we synthesize the students strengths and the needs of multiple stakeholders to inform a comprehensive HMW question for our new curriculum? The more scrutiny of our stakeholders we undertake, the more potent our question will be for unleashing our creative ideation.

This model isn't intended to replace your curriculum mapping template. It is intended to help your team think divergently to consider and ultimately choose ways to complete that template that are unique and transformative of teaching and learning in your district. Whether you use a phenomena-based approach or essential questions and learning targets, a design thinking mindset and model will help you entertain learning experiences you might not have considered otherwise. It can also help you to think differently about the standards that are the basis for your units. Furthermore, the HMW question stem can help you to frame questions in ways that inherently invite student participation in not just finding, but executing an answer. Instead of a civics question such as "How are decisions made in a democracy?" Students could ask, "How might we include more diverse points of view in the decision-making process?" Now they aren't bystanders to decision making, they are decision makers.

STEP 4 IS TO DEVELOP A PROTOTYPE OF OUR BEST IDEA, FOLLOWED BY STEPS 5 AND 6 WHERE YOU TEST AND ITERATE ON THAT DESIGN BASED ON USER FEEDBACK

Applying this part of design to curriculum writing is likely the biggest departure from the processes you have previously used. Working in a space with your collaborative thought partners surrounded by white boards full of ideas, post-it notes, and sharpies, the idea on which your thinking has converged seems awesome. This moment of collective excitement about where your problem solving is headed is a priceless one because at this moment, after all of your research and brainstorming and yes, and-ing, it is hard to imagine someone—anyone—not liking what you are building. This is why a prototype, or a minimum viable product (MVP), is so important. This most basic model of the product you vision is necessary so that before you are too far down the development path you test your idea on real users; you find out if they want what you are designing and if they will use what you are building.

Prototypes can take many forms. Perhaps what comes to mind when you read that word is a new version of a backpack made from cardboard or the pipe cleaner and popsicle stick models from a maker space. Maybe those maker space models are animated with Little Bits. If you are old enough to remember Fred Flintstone's car, that too, is much like a prototype. A prototype is a model of an idea that gives beta testers an understanding of how the final product will function or the service it will provide. A prototype is meant to be discarded. A prototype for an app can be a paper version of the possible screens; when a beta tester taps the icon for the button on the paper screen, the designer presents the paper version of the next screen that would appear. The designer can ask questions of the tester: Why did you click there? What did you expect would happen? Or even, is that button where you expected it would be? Later in Case 11 you will read about Jen De Lisi-Hall's app and her beta test versions. Her first MVP was just a Google Sheet!

Think back on a recent curriculum writing experience you had. After you had identified the standards you would address in a unit, the unit essential question, learning targets, etc., could your team have benefited from stakeholder input? If you were revising the curriculum for a currently existing course, how might the process have been positively influenced by testing it on students who had completed the curriculum in its previous iteration? If you were writing a new course, who might the stakeholders be, and what kind of insight might you gain from testing a prototype with them?

A curriculum isn't a car or a backpack. You can't build a tangible thing out of cardboard or Legos. Unless you are building an online learning experience, a digital prototype or paper app screens aren't the way to go either. So how might a curriculum prototype work? Another method of prototyping is to create an experience. Create a video commercial for your course. What would the course "movie trailer" look and sound like? What highlights of the curriculum would you emphasize to show stakeholders you created this learning experience with them in mind? Could you create a mock lesson and role play how the curriculum would be implemented and show how learning is engaging and the content has real-world meaning and application? Even if the curriculum you are writing is being mandated by a higher educational authority, that is simply a constraint. Where in the design process can you find room to reflect the needs and interests of your stakeholders, and when and how can you get their feedback?

The purpose of the feedback at this stage in your design is to iterate before you deliver the product. On an episode of the podcast, *Clever*, when interviewing

David Schwartz of HUSH studios, Designer Amy Devers commented that you can't cut a board and make it longer! I found that to be an amusing adaptation of the old proverb, "measure twice, cut once." Wisdom that applies to the built world, applies to our design as educators as well. User feedback—from parents at open house night, students in our classrooms every day, colleagues with whom we collaborate—is an essential component of purposeful responsive iteration. Feedback as part of a design cycle is not criticism or judgment. Design is messy and challenging. Candid feedback is the fodder for increasingly effective problem solving, for deeper empathy, and building the creative ideation muscles we all have.

Notes

They worked to solve a real problem that we live with. In the big problem they see the purpose of the math we are studying. They bring lots of ideas to the table.

5

Human-Centered Collaboration: Colleagues as Designers

How Might We Enhance Student Learning through Transdisciplinary Colleague Collaboration?

In this chapter, we are returning to our teacher personas: Cheryl, Julie, Darren, and Kai, and adding other potential collaboration partners for this section: Mitch (a school counselor), Lois (a teacher-librarian), Gloria (an assistant principal), and Stanley (an athletic director). As we embark on building collaborative partnerships with our colleagues, we can learn something from interior designer Ilse Crawford, who takes an empathy-driven approach to her work designing space and furniture. Crawford reminds her team: we have two eyes, two ears, and one mouth. We must use them in that proportion. In fact, Crawford spends several months getting to know her clients so that when she begins to ideate she is intimately aware of their needs, and those needs inform her design choices. (Note: If you are interested in Crawford and her process, I recommend the profile of her in season 1, episode 8, of the Netflix series, *Abstract: The Art of Design*.)

Whether you are a brand new member of your learning community still trying to remember everyone's name or a twenty-five-year veteran who has attended weddings, happy hours, and social gatherings with your colleagues for a quarter century, Crawford's advice is the best starting point for peer collaboration. It likely comes as no surprise to know that as a library media specialist, my most frequent collaboration was with social studies and English teachers. Periodically, I ventured into new territory with other departments, one time coplanning a unit with a chemistry teacher. She contacted me because, as the teacher of AP Chemistry, she always had remaining class sessions between the administration of the AP exam and the end of our school year. She was hoping I could help her plan something meaningful and interesting for her students. She was willing to think about it as "found time."

Our conversation became a twofold exercise in applying design thinking! First, I put aside the different ideas that were bouncing around my head, things I thought might interest the students, although I certainly didn't know the students as well as she did. Instead of offering suggestions (which actually is what she hoped I would do when she came to me), I started asking her questions:

- What outcome would make her think the time was well spent?
- What difficulties did she have this year when teaching the class?
- Or what difficulty had the students had?

As I listened to her reflect about her year, I gained empathy with her as a teacher, as a teacher of a specific discipline, and as a teacher of a particular high-stakes course. That helped me to hear things she was saying, like: "It's more my Honors Chemistry students [an entirely different class] who have trouble with some of the concepts of their class, but I don't have time for a big project with them."

I asked her, "Do you have enough time to ask the Honors Chem students to share what areas or concepts caused them the most difficulty?" She said that she didn't have to ask, she knew.

I pushed again by saying, "Your insight about their struggle is really important, and could you put together a form that asks them to tell you, in their words, about these struggles? It would be interesting to see their self-awareness." She agreed that would be an interesting comparison.

Then I asked, "How might we harness the found time in AP to empower the AP students to help the Honors class finish the year strong and prepare for their final exam?" And a project was born! Later, in Chapter 6, we will return to this project. If your curiosity has been piqued, go there now to read about the project, and see if you can adopt and adapt any of it for your students. In fact, ask your students to read about the project, and then ask them to reflect on how and whether such an experience would help them. If they think it might, pose an HMW question to them. Something like: How might we leverage each other's learning strengths to improve our mastery of the units where we struggle? Or, how might we create and implement found time in our course of study? Then, come back to this section and practice empathizing with the educator personas in order to identify opportunities for collaboration with your colleagues.

UNPACKING A TEACHER PERSONA: JULIE

As we did with the student stakeholder in Chapter 4, we will consider a couple of the educator personas as models for embarking on collaborative adventures.

For this exercise, we will be working with one of these personas to address a problem we confront in our school. I want to emphasize, the problem is not the colleague persona, it is an institutional or community issue that impacts all of us in the school, for example: teacher retention, implicit bias, the mental wellness of the members of the learning community, controversial politics in the classroom, purposeful teaching with technology, cyberbullying, budget cuts, etc.

I hope you find a persona that resonates with you because it reflects one of your colleagues and helps you to begin the process of gaining empathy with him/her/them so that you can co-construct projects or partner to solve problems that face your learning community. We will start by examining a classroom-based colleague and then spend some time with an educator in a nonclassroom role. As you undertake this exercise, I invite you to choose a persona that challenges you: is it the veteran teacher who is being outpaced by technology? Or the new-to-teaching teacher who seems rather overwhelmed adjusting to the job? Maybe it is the teacher of color who is feeling isolated from the faculty. Review Figure 4.1, Understand Your Stakeholder, the "brain" graphic from Chapter 4; then on the next pages are two completed versions that examine Julie, the veteran teacher. The first one has the think, say, feel, do sections filled in (see Figure 5.1), and the need section is empty. Try your hand at interpreting Julie's needs. The next graphic includes an interpretation of Julie's needs that might help you increase your empathy with her (see Figure 5.2).

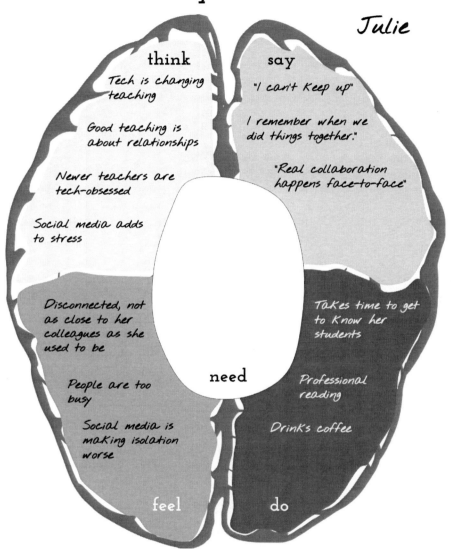

FIGURE 5.1 Teacher (Julie) Completed

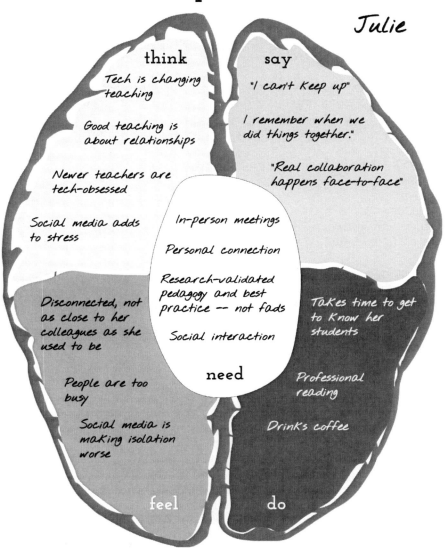

FIGURE 5.2 Julie's Needs

Let's take on the challenge of collegial collaboration. That seems to be a problem that Julie (like many of us) faces and one that could invite exposure to meaningful implementation of instructional technology as well. We start with our problem statement:

> Julie needs support incorporating instructional technology into her planning because she thinks technology is eroding interpersonal relationships.

Embedded in this statement are some of our insights about Julie that, with a little more examination, might yield assets we can leverage. Consider this:

- Julie likes her students, her colleagues, professional growth, and coffee.
- Julie knows she is good at building relationships with people.
- Julie wishes that people would take more time to get to know each other.

And equipped with these insights, we can start to think about our "How might we . . ." question.

- How might we reimagine required, face-to-face meetings in order to create more social environments for professional learning?
- How might we assemble professional learning teams in order to help teachers get to know each other?
- How might we create instructional opportunities for teachers to collaborate?

If you are up for the challenge, this is a good time to examine some of the other personas and determine if the needs we have identified in our consideration of Julie appear other places in our learning community. Darren, the new-to-teaching teacher says that he is sometimes dismissed as a tech-obsessed millennial, so he intersects with Julie rather dramatically in terms of relationships and technology perceptions. Similarly, Kai feels alienated from his new colleagues because of diversity issues. Like Darren, he is new to the school, and like Julie, he is a veteran teacher. And like both of them he needs to build better relationships with his colleagues.

When we examine the other faculty members, the pattern continues. Mitch, the school counselor, feels underappreciated by his colleagues, who don't understand the scope of his role. Lois, the teacher-librarian, has a similar experience. Gloria, the new assistant principal, is concerned about how her collegial relationships have been affected by her transition from teaching to administration. There is definitely a pattern here.

Here is a challenge for your design team: each member of your team can unpack one of the faculty personas using Figure 4.1, Understand Your Stakeholder. Then, compare the needs you identify and find possible commonality. Then, look for insights, motivations, and assets in what the personas say, do, think, and feel. Can you leverage their passions and talents in a "How might we . . ." question that addresses their shared problem? Of course you can!

Ideation: The Divergent Thinking Phase

We have now been through two examples of the early stages of the design process. We have spent time considering a couple of the personas as stakeholders in our learning community. By examining their words, actions, thoughts, and feelings, we developed a nuanced understanding of the problem we are trying to solve and crafted potent "How might we . . ." questions. It is now time for ideation or brainstorming possible solutions.

Ideation is about divergent thinking. It requires being nonjudgmentally open to possibilities. It requires the brain power of a team—the "we" in how might we—to push the ideation beyond what we already know to do and into the realm of creating something new, untried, and revelatory. Keep that in mind as you continue reading about possible responses to the problem of eroding colleague connectedness. When you read the solutions explored here, you may say, "Good idea, but that won't work at my school." I respond to that statement with "Why?" And to your answer with another "Why?" I will respond with the question "Why?" five times. This examination technique is called "The Five Whys." Likely, once we have completed the five cycles, we will have exposed the habits of past practice and culture that interfere with many potential solutions so that they can be removed or overcome. Or we may have uncovered an alternative solution that is inspired by the one that doesn't seem possible. Try it! It is a thought-provoking and idea-liberating process. It helps to get at the root causes of problems that may still elude you in your designing. Regardless, your team's solution to your learning communities challenge must respond to the real people who are invested in your plan. The ideas here are simply a starting point for how you might think about similar issues at your school. Take them as the inspiration they are intended to be and not a recipe for the solution you should implement.

BRAINSTORMING TO MEET JULIE'S NEEDS

We are going to combine two brainstorming techniques here, Crazy 8s and "Yes! And. . . ." Here's how they work: for Crazy 8s you need paper and a marker. A good size is 11×17 because it gives enough ideation space without crowding people sitting at a table. It is important to use marker (I won't assign a brand name to it) because with a marker you must make bold and definitive marks on the paper, and then your brain will just go with it. No pencils. No erasing. No barely legible marks. Fold the paper in half three times. See Figure 5.3.

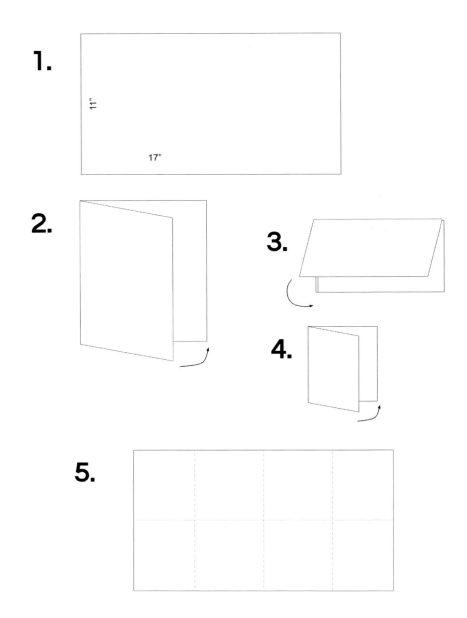

FIGURE 5.3 Crazy 8s Paper Fold

Next, set a timer for 40 seconds. That is how much time you have to capture one idea in one box on the paper. When the timer goes off, start it again and move to the next box. Keep going, eight times, until each of the eight spaces on the paper is full. When you are done, it will look something like Figure 5.4.

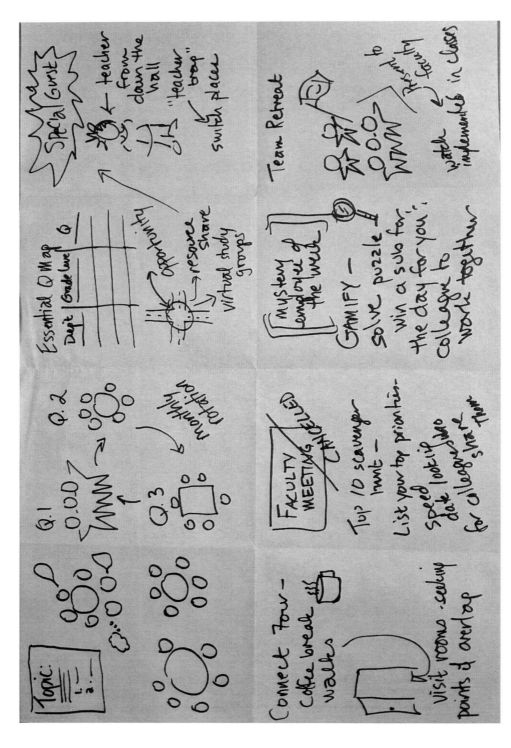

FIGURE 5.4 Crazy 8s Peer Collaboration

Share your ideas with another member of your design team so they can give you NWH feedback. Which ideas are your "N" ideas? You can do it right now. It will be an easy, low-stakes win. How about "W" or Wow! ideas? That's a cool concept, but it will require a bit of planning, and we can totally do that. Do you have any "H" ideas? Those are the ideas that will have a big impact; it just isn't immediately apparent how you might make it happen. "How" ideas require you to draw upon your learning community resources and end up being transformative experiences. Questions that begin with how are just problems waiting to be solved!

Once you and your partner have given each other feedback, you are ready to "Yes! And . . ." one of the ideas into greatness! This technique is an improv practice. One member of the ensemble throws an idea into the skit, and another cast member validates the idea (Yes!) before building on the idea (And . . .) so that the scene evolves. For example:

Wow. The sky sure is dark.

It sure is! And, it looks like the stars are starting to shine.

It did look like stars at first. And now those lights are changing colors.

Whoa—so many different colors. And now they are sending down beams to earth!

I hope you get the idea. This is what your design team can do next. Choose one of your ideas. Maybe you start with a "Wow!" idea. State your idea, and then your partner replies with: "Yes! And . . ." in order to add to the starting idea. Then you say, "Yes! And . . . [insert your next idea here]." See how far you can go building on each other's ideas and what new creative solutions emerge. As an alternative, you can have the whole team "Yes! And" one idea. And then another, and another . . .

Prototyping: Ideas Come to Life

A prototype is simply a rudimentary expression or model of the solution you are exploring. Whatever form it takes, you only need to build enough that your beta testers can try it out, understand how it is supposed to work, and critique it for you. Prototypes (see Figure 5.5) are intended to end up in the recycle bin. When a design team is prototyping a physical product, it is useful to have rudimentary materials. I keep small bins of pipe cleaners, toothpicks and popsicle sticks, duct tape, cardboard, aluminum foil, markers, and scrap paper around my workspace for these exercises.

Sometimes you are prototyping an idea. In those situations it can be useful to write a 60-second skit that portrays your school when the solution has been implemented and taken effect. In other words, life after the problem has been eliminated, and the solution you devised is the new reality. Similarly, you can use a program like Adobe Spark to build a sequence of still images

46 Student-Centered Learning by Design

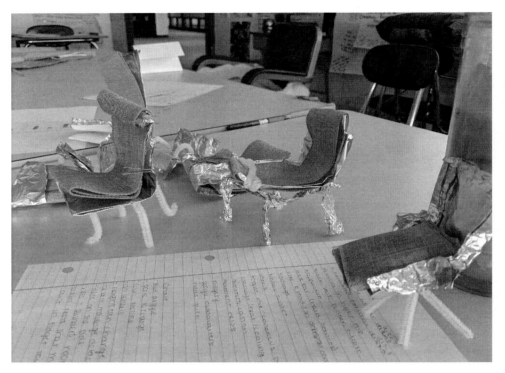

FIGURE 5.5 Chair Prototypes

over which you narrate the story of how life at your school was transformed by your solution. Another version of this prototype can be created by drawing each scene in a storyboard—or even on sticky notes—and then record a narration of the scenes with your phone. Figure 5.6 is an example of what a storyboard prototype can look like.

This link bit.ly/VidProto goes to the video made from Figure 5.6 storyboard. When you watch the video, notice the arc of the story. It is likely very familiar to you. It is the story arc used by the PIXAR teams when they draft and pitch story ideas. It goes like this:

Once upon a time . . .

Everyday . . .

Until one day . . .

Because of that . . .

Because of that . . .

Until finally . . .

FIGURE 5.6 Stickies Storyboard

An alternative to this story framework is the hero's journey depicted in Figure 5.7. Be sure to cast your hero, your helper, the challengers, and the tempters carefully. The goal of the prototype is to find out if people are interested in your solution, if they will use or try it, and where it works and where it breaks. In other words, do they want it? Will they use it?

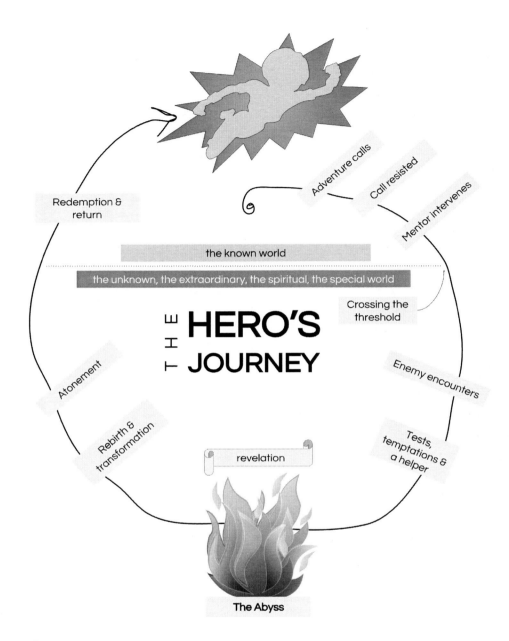

FIGURE 5.7 Hero's Journey

Feedback on your prototype should send you back to the proverbial drawing board. Design is an iterative process. You started with the needs of one stakeholder, like Benjamin or Julie, and now you are extrapolating from that person to build a solution to a problem many people are experiencing. Their feedback, not just Benjamin's or Julie's, is an essential component to enhancing your design to maximum impact. I provided you with multiple personas so that you can practice understanding multiple stakeholders, looking for common ground in their experiences on which you can build, and identifying their unique needs that must be met to promote the success of your idea. When we see solutions to problems in this way—iterative in response to feedback—we are shifting our mindset to being comfortable with change. I think, in our hearts, we know that the world is not static. We know that Gordon Moore (see the discussion of Moore's law in Chapter 4) was right about the pace of change. As the Fourth Industrial Revolution courses through all the systems of our lives disrupting how we do what we do, it is only logical that how and what we teach will continue to shift. A human-centered design mindset is an adaptation to thriving at the pace of change.

Notes

We so often are reactive to situations in our classrooms with discipline referral slips when the solutions to problems can live in our own classrooms, with the students who are experiencing the situations.

6

Learning by Design: Putting Students at the Center as Design Thinkers

How Might We Disrupt the Traditional Classroom Structure to Empower Students to Be Agents of Change and to Take Informed Action?

This chapter is a collection of examples of human-centered design implemented by educators working with students of different ages. In some cases, colleagues (like a classroom teacher and a teacher-librarian) collaborated to facilitate the experience. In others, one classroom teacher worked alone with his/her/their students. The goal or outcome, in each case, was the disruption of a traditional approach to a unit or assessment in order to increase student investment in the learning opportunity. As we unpack and celebrate each project or experience, we will align the learning process with the needs of the student personas. When we put students at the center of the learning, by design, we increase their engagement and deepen their learning. We meet their needs as learners and as people.

CASE 1: HIGH SCHOOL SOCIOLOGY CLASS

How might we disrupt senioritis?

Remember our student persona, Benjamin? Keep him in mind as you read about high school social studies teacher Michelle Maher and the approach she and I used when trying to decide: how might we disrupt senioritis? Michelle taught two sections of sociology. The students in the classes were all seniors, and the semester is a bit abbreviated since the seniors work at internships for the last month of school. We met a couple of times to discuss the challenges she was confronting:

- Second-semester seniors can be an engagement challenge.
- Our contentious civic climate means some of the course topics are challenging to discuss.
- Teaching the same course for the six semesters in a row means a teacher is challenged to keep it fresh and relevant.

Getting Started

Our partnership was exciting! Michelle is my pedagogical soul mate. She thinks ten times about any curricular idea. She is a model of risk-taking in the classroom. Failure is always forward, so it isn't really a failure at all. Given these habits of mind, we started with a blank slate and this question:

How might we disrupt senioritis and ignite students' passion for working on solutions to social issues?

And then we wondered: where do we start when we have a blank slate?

We began with our general musings about how to personalize this study, how to help students wrap their heads around the macro and micro views of sociology. Addiction is an issue that lends itself to sociological study on a macro level, and juuling at a high school is a micro view. Gender is a macro topic; professional training of teachers around issues of gender identity in the classroom is more micro. The more we talked, the more it became clear that the students were going to have autonomy over their focus for the semester, and their purpose was going to be to apply their skills to solving a community problem. The question was: How?

Embracing the principles of Universal Design for Learning (UDL), we considered how to remove barriers to student engagement, content access, and their expressions of learning. We discussed how to promote divergent and convergent thinking processes to encourage students to think of societal issues in both macro and micro ways and invite them to see connections between the different topics.

We continued brainstorming. What if we present them with an artifact (inspired by the Q-focus from the Right Question Institute's QFT protocol documented in *Make Just One Change* by Dan Rothstein and Luz Santana) and have them list on one side of the artifact all of the macro issues related to it, and on the other side list all the micro issues indicated by it. Then we thought about showing them these two videos for the purpose of macro-micro comparisons:

First: Dove's ad about beauty standards and young girls: bit.ly/Dovebeauty

And then: Greenpeace's response: bit.ly/gpresponse

And here was the rub. These students didn't have experience really owning their learning. They had been given choice, as in make this product or that product, but they hadn't been given complete autonomy over any learning experience. Realizing that we were already flexing our design thinking muscles trying to empathize with this group of students and design an approach to the course that would meet their needs, we decided that we needed to guide them through this same process so each student could meaningfully chart his/her/their own path through the curriculum.

To figure out what this would look like, we turned to the Future Design School (futuredesignschool.com) iPad app which has a Design Thinking for High School Students curriculum. Everything my colleague needed to confidently facilitate her classes adopting the mindset of innovators and successfully navigate this personalized experience is included. We were prepared to challenge them to identify macro societal problems, focus them to the micro school or community level, and then engage in the necessary work of empathizing with their peers and fellow community members to research, design, test, and iterate the best possible solution to these shared problems.

The Design Sprint

Because we were concerned about student buy-in, we thought it would help the students if they knew where this was all going, as in what does "the design process" mean soup-to-nuts? What are we in for? To that end, we decided to do a design sprint with them: the whole process in 45 minutes. Drawing on my experience at the Google Certified Innovator Academy, we decided to have one class design a chair and the other design a wallet. In each class, I was the stakeholder; the students were all designing to meet my needs. In each class I stood in the center of the room and told a story. To one class I told the story of traveling ten years ago and being pickpocketed and needing to replace my wallet. Now that wallet was wearing out, and my wallet needs had changed dramatically. The class began peppering me with questions about my shopping habits, about my phone, about my acceptance of or aversion to change (the state of being, not the coins—we had to clarify), about my likes and dislikes, about how my life has evolved over the last ten years. In the other class I told a tale of woe about aging, body breakdown and injuries and the impact all of that has on sitting. Again they questioned me and asked about reading and computer routines and other lifestyle habits.

54 Student-Centered Learning by Design

After these intense Q&A sessions, the students were each given the following materials:

- One piece of 8.5 × 11 scrap paper
- One piece (roughly the same size) of aluminum foil
- A single pipe cleaner
- A piece of wire-edged ribbon about 6 inches long

They were given 5 minutes to build the perfect wallet or chair to suit my needs. At the end of 5 minutes each student was paired with a student across the room. They were each given 30 seconds to pitch their design to their partner. At the end of a minute, they chose which of their two designs was best, set the other aside, and became a team pitching the winning prototype to another newly formed team. We continued the process of pitch, choose, set aside, merge, and re-pitch until they were down to two designs. They then pitched to me. I critiqued each design and then chose the one that best met my needs.

Reflection on the Sprint

Michelle and I then guided a reflective discussion about the experience. Organically, the students acknowledged some important elements of the design process:

Empathy:
They all realized that they were intently focused on me the whole time. When they pitched, it was about being best at meeting my needs. They never judged me or disregarded something I said, and they never presumed to know me better than I know myself and my needs.

Collaboration:
Each time they regrouped their pitch improved when new voices helped explain the product. And when I was critiquing prototypes at the end, they realized that most of the features I wanted were in some design somewhere in the room. If they worked together, they could have combined those features into the best possible design. Additionally, the students were aware that Michelle and I were collaborating to facilitate this exercise. When her content expertise and my design thinking experience were integrated, the lesson for the students was much richer than what either of us would have facilitated alone. And, the students watched us talk, reflect, revise, and share the stage, so to speak. Think about it: we frequently ask students to collaborate and what they are actually doing (and maybe what we actually mean) is cooperate, as Michael Cohen says. Students don't have many opportunities to have collaboration—a team working together to create and deliver something none of them could accomplish alone—in action. Absent such a model, their cooperative work is parallel play, not an integrated and interdependent learning experience.

Iteration:
Without either of us saying anything, both classes said they could make a new design where they could combine their best ideas into one chair (or wallet),

maybe use better materials, and test it again. And they also realized that talking to me with a prototype in their hand elicited important insight into my needs and how to satisfy them. They wanted more information. They were designing with me.

The Students' Turn

At this point, it was time for Michelle and her students to return to the content of the course. Together, Michelle and I brainstormed strategies that we could share with the students to help them identify a societal issue that authentically concerns and engages them and begin the process of defining the problem and finding the stakeholders who experience it. Design thinking as pedagogy is empowering for both educators and students. Ultimately, Michelle offered students several paths for identifying as many topics as possible. We showed them a couple of Google Trend's "Year in Search" videos (bit.ly/Yis2019) and directed them to current issue topic collections in the library's databases. We directed them to write the issues on sticky notes (one issue per note), and then we collected them on the wall outside the classroom. Then, they began the process of sorting the issues into three categories: global, national, and local. As they sorted, they added to the categories. Ultimately, Michelle wanted them to each choose an issue from the local category, and this approach helped them see how the issues they face in their community, connect them with people in other parts of the country and around the world.

We moved this exercise to the hallway to give students space to move and think, to flexibly regroup with one another and discuss their ideas, and to generally break old habits associated with sitting at their desks in the class. Taking this part of the exercise to the hallway also invited people outside of the class to participate in the conversations we were having. Some people asked what we were doing and could they join. Some students who were wandering by tried to distract their friends who were in class. Rather than shooing them away, we invited them to help us brainstorm. Interesting conversations were happening about the problems we collectively face. Most importantly, when one student would say something like: that problem is huge and we are going to do anything to fix it, other students responded: even if we can't fix the huge problem, we can do something about the local one, and that is a step in the process. Something really important was happening: the students who were accustomed to being passive recipients of content were learning to see opportunity in the challenges and themselves as active agents of change.

Real-World Research

Enter, the teacher-librarian. For our purposes, that is the persona of Lois. Figure 6.1 is the understand your stakeholder graphic completed with Lois as the focus. Review that graphic, and notice all that Lois says and does that equips her to be an asset to the work the students are going to do as they set out to validate the problem they want to solve and empathize with the people (in some cases their peers) who live with the problem on a day-to-day basis.

Furthermore, notice how many of Lois's professional needs can be met through this partnership. Many of our frustrations as educators are rooted in a sense of isolation we develop due to the structures of our schools. Human-centered design pedagogy is inherently collaborative, so it naturally helps to build connections and relationships and erode isolation.

Purposeful and prolonged collaboration between the classroom teacher and the teacher-librarian cuts in half the student-teacher ratio in a class. Consider the ramifications of that for teaching and learning! More consistent and immediate feedback to students on their work, more opportunities to meet students' individual skill and interest needs, more support for students pursuing a wide range of topics rather than one prescribed, more stimulation for educators' creative thinking, and support—across the board—for everyone's increased risk-taking.

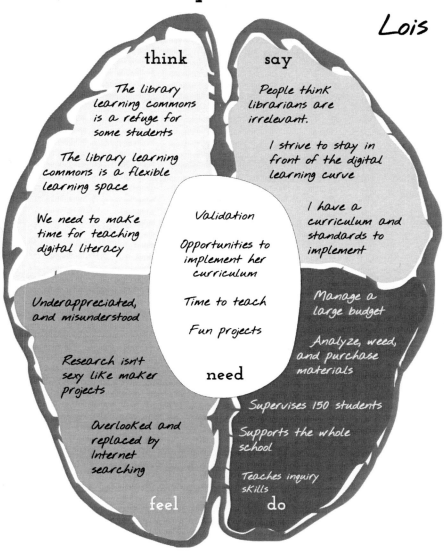

FIGURE 6.1 Librarian (Lois) Completed

CASE 2: DIGITAL LITERACY CLASS

How might we solve problems of social media while preserving its benefits?

When you read about this three-week unit, keep student persona Adrian in mind. In fact, before reading, you might want to try your hand at completing an "understand your stakeholder" organizer (Figure 4.1) about Adrian; then write a problem statement, and identify resources and insights you uncover about him (Figure 4.3). When you read about this unit, consider how and whether this learning experience might have helped, interested, or empowered him in some way.

I facilitated this unit in a class I designed and taught called Digital Literacy; I called the unit "Social: The New Media." I curated a playlist of videos on YouTube for creating flipped lessons and giving students opportunities to explore subtopics of interest to them. I consulted the lessons and ideas published by SHEG, the Stanford History Education Group, who conducted the watershed 2016 study on students' civic online reasoning skills (you can read that report here, bit.ly/SHEGreport, and see their collection of classroom exercises here, cor.stanford.edu). I also curated from Google's Applied Digital Skills (bit.ly/ADSgoogle) and "The Sift" newsletter (bit.ly/NLPSift) from the *News Literacy Project*. Clearly, I had lots of stuff I could ask the students to do, but I was owning it and that didn't feel right.

So I put everything to the side, cleared off my desk, and got blank paper and some sharpies. Get ready for Crazy 8s! I started to think about problems I hear people lament about social media. Not because I want to make a case for my students that social media is rotting their brains and they need to do something healthier with their time. Frankly, that would be quite hypocritical of me! Instead, I decided we would set out to solve the problems.

Here is how it worked in practice.

First, I covered tables with paper, piled a bunch of sharpies and markers in the middle, and let each student claim a spot as s/he arrived. With five or six students at each table, in the center of the tables, I wrote this question: "What Is Social Media?"

The lesson on the first day unfolded in four phases.

Phase 1: Defining
- Round 1: Write your definition of social media on the table where you are sitting.
- Round 2: Rotate clockwise, read what you find, and add to or amend it. Do not cross out or cover anything you find.

Phase 2: Pros
- Round 3: Rotate again, read what you find, and make a list of the "pros" of social media. What are the benefits?
- Round 4a: Rotate, and, once again, read what you find and add to the list without covering or removing anything you find already there.

Phase 3: Cons
- Round 4b: Now start a list of "cons" when you think about social media. What are the drawbacks or detriments?
- Round 5: Rotate one last time, and now you are back where you started. Read what you find. Add anything you want. And then, circle the pro that matters most to you and the con that most bothers you.

Before moving to the next phase, we discussed the process we had just used and how it mimics social media posting and commenting. We considered why I asked them to only respond to previous comments and be sure to not write over or cross any out. We also talked about how or whether they filtered what they wrote because it was on the table where I could see it and it felt "permanent" doing it with sharpies. A little nod to digital citizenship.

Phase 4: How Might We
- Round 6: Write your "How might we . . ." question. How might we preserve (your pro) while fixing (your con)?

Figure 6.2 is what a table looked like at the end of the lesson.
And here are some of their "How might we . . ." questions:

HMW preserve a way to connect and share ideas while fixing a false sense of success?
HMW preserve the connection between others while fixing the distribution of hate?
HMW preserve the freedom of being able to share what we want and being able to connect with others while fixing the consumption of time it takes?
HMW preserve social media's ability to connect us with varied communities while fixing the way it encourages dangerous comparisons?
HMW preserve connecting with friends while fixing the spreading of hate and false information?

Day 2 was all about growing empathy with social media users other than ourselves. The students started this process by thinking about someone they know who has experienced the social media problem they are addressing. They listed all they know about that person: what they do, what they say about themselves and about social media, etc. Then, they wrote three open-ended questions they could ask that person to learn more about that person's experiences with social media. And then they conducted interviews. Some students called people on the phone and discussed their topic while taking notes on what their subject said. Others went to other parts of the school to find people. Others sent emails.

At the end of the class, they all came back to our classroom to review their interview notes. They highlighted anything that their subject(s) said that was interesting, enlightening, or new information that they didn't already know about the person. These insights were used to refine their "How might we . . ."

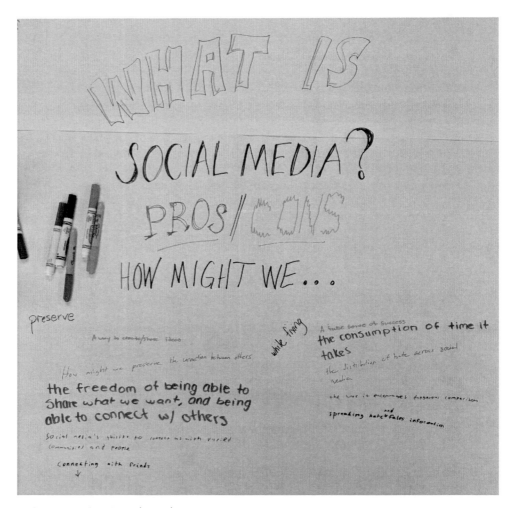

FIGURE 6.2 Social Media HMW

questions to more accurately reflect the needs of the people they interviewed and inspire a productive ideation process.

Remember all of the resources that I collected in preparation for teaching this unit? That time spent was not all for naught because at this point those materials were excellent sources for the students as they began to research possible solutions to the problems they were tackling. And, now they were invested in reading, watching, and unpacking these resources because they weren't just assignments for class—they were potential keys to the solutions they were developing. Ultimately, this learning process, over which the students had agency, was much more meaningful and empowering than any teacher-directed instruction I could have created.

Learning by Design   61

Time for Ideation

Once the students each had a "How might we . . ." (HMW) question, they were ready for the next design thinking step: ideation. On two occasions earlier during this course, we used Crazy 8s, and for this experience I wanted to expose them to a new brainstorming technique. I chose a round robin approach because that process would continue emulating social media posting, which was the focus of our problem solving.

We started out with blank paper covering the table. Each student wrote their HMW question across the bottom of the paper at their spot at the table. Then, they began to draw what a solution to their problem might look like. They could use a combination of words and graphics to convey their vision. We spent 15 minutes drawing ideas, and the room was silent almost the whole time. At one point, one student said, "I'm not sure . . ." and then trailed off. I responded by saying: "Try drawing what it would be like if your problem didn't exist."

After 15 minutes we rotated seats. I asked the students to review the idea captured on the paper in front of them and then add to it. I said they could add clarifying questions about elements they were not sure if they understood; they could add ideas in the form or words and drawings. The only thing they couldn't do was cross anything off the page. Once an idea was written or drawn, it was there to stay—just like social media. The only thing I

FIGURE 6.3   Group Brainstorm

did allow students to cross out was something they had written—there was no erasing other people's thoughts. And, we were all working in pen or marker so even cross outs left a trail. In this way, our pen-and-paper process emulated social media posting. We stayed at our new seats for several minutes to give each student ample time to reflect and contribute before rotating again.

With six students at a table, the midpoint of the exercise was after the third rotation. At this point we stopped to reflect on the process. I directed the students to talk about what they were doing and how that compared with their typical role or conduct in class. I asked them not to talk about the ideas on the paper, just to talk about what they were doing, how they felt, or what they thought about the process. I was struck when my student who was most anxious about contributing to class discussions said that she had time to thoroughly consider her ideas and write them carefully so that they would make sense. She remarked that when she tries to talk in class she gets wrapped up in her thoughts and can't articulate her ideas clearly. But with this process she had a lot to say. How cool?! And a happy by-product that I didn't anticipate.

We continued rotating seats and adding ideas until everyone returned to their original spot. Figure 6.3 shows what the brainstorming work of a group looked like. We ended class with students sharing with the group how their idea was evolving and collecting for themselves follow-up questions they wanted to ask the group during the next class.

Prototype and User Testing

The students had a few options for how to proceed with building their prototype. They could use cardboard and other basic supplies from our maker space to build a 3D object. They could use paper templates to design or redesign an app. Or, they could storyboard the experience of their solution in action by drawing the sequences on post-its and creating a short video. We looked at examples of low-tech prototypes such as backpacks assembled from cardboard and discussed how they needed to build just enough so that a beta tester could understand the purpose of what they were creating and simulate how it would work. I kept reminding them that the prototypes would ultimately end up being recycled once they had served their function.

When it came time for user testing the students met one-on-one with members of our school community to watch how those people interacted with their prototypes, and they were able to interview those users about their reactions to the proposed solution both in terms of the viability of the concept and its appeal. To prepare for these testing sessions, each student decided whether to test if users wanted their product or how their product would work and wrote two or three questions to ask their users as they watched them use the prototype.

In order to solicit a broader spectrum of perspectives, each of the students uploaded their design to a Google Form, which they used to ask key questions about their design. Then I added each Form to a Padlet (padlet.com) that we shared through our social media networks in order to reach a wider audience of social media users and increase the perspectives provided in the feedback. This authentic audience pushed students to step up their prototype presentation game; many of them were surprised to receive feedback, and several commented that they wanted to improve their designs and try again. The process naturally took over. We concluded our unit with a pitchfest. We invited their original stakeholder and beta testers as well as other teachers and administrators in the building to watch them pitch their final ideas and provide them with a last round of feedback. The unit ended and their iterative thinking continued.

CASE 3: ADVANCED PLACEMENT CHEMISTRY

How might we leverage found time to amplify student-directed learning?

Here we return to the conversation I had with the AP Chemistry teacher. If you would like a point of reference, this teacher has a lot in common with the persona, Cheryl. The chemistry teacher with whom I collaborated on this exercise is the picture of enthusiasm. She is invested in each of her students as people, not just students. She is the champion of faculty connectedness, frequently organizing small and large social opportunities for teachers to bond and form community. She is loved and respected by both her students and her colleagues.

When we left this story back in Chapter 5, we had developed our first HMW question: "How might we harness the found time in AP to empower the AP students to help the Honors Chem class finish the year strong and prepare for their final exam?"

With this question as our focus, the teacher and I started, organically, thinking 10X and growing the idea with "Yes! And. . . ." It went like this:

- "We can start by giving a survey to the Honors Chem classes . . ."
- "Yes! And, we can ask each AP student to choose to work on one of the problems that emerges from their survey responses."
- "Yes! And, they can interview the students in Honors to understand why that concept was difficult."
- "Yes! And, the AP students can build new teaching materials for the students to use to practice the concept before they take their final exam."
- "Yes! And, next year those materials can be used again to differentiate the original instruction for the new class!"

That was the first layer of design thinking that we undertook together. The cool thing is that the product of that planning session was to put the AP classes through a design thinking exercise as the path to developing their solution to the learning problems of their peers! My colleague asked for reassurance that I would be with her (and her students) throughout the process. She also asked a bunch of "what if" questions. Mostly they were about what if something goes wrong. I asked, what do the AP classes lose if their projects flop? Not much really. What does the Honors class lose? Again, nothing. They don't gain anything, but very little of their time and energy is invested in the project. They are the beneficiaries if all goes well. I then asked if she would lose anything if all goes awry. She didn't hesitate to say, not really. She likes her students (and they like her); she considers them eager learners, thoughtful people, and she trusts them. Ultimately, she realized that if this flops, they will be rather forgiving. That is when I felt safe to tell her it won't flop. It may evolve differently than we anticipate, and that is OK. In fact, iteration is part of the process and how things improve in response to the needs that are uncovered through interviews, observations, and research. Ultimately, everyone stands to gain much more than anyone stands to lose. And then she asked if I could write up the unit plan.

So here is the project outline (see Figures 6.4 and 6.5) that the students in AP Chem students followed.

The AP exam is over. (Phew!) **The final lab is complete.** (YES!)

Now we have the gifts of **found time**, sophisticated **chemistry expertise**, and a cohort of **innovative risk-takers**. Here is how we will use these gifts to solve problems and keep learning ourselves:

To start, we will survey the grade 10 students in Honors Chem. What we want to know about each student is:

- What was the hardest content or skill for you to master this year?
- Or, looking ahead to the final exam, what potential questions or problems most concern you?

This is where YOU, the students in AP Chem enter the equation. Each of you will choose one of the issues identified by your 10th grade peers and design a learning module to help them overcome their struggle. You will use this guiding design question to frame your work:

**How might we create learning experiences
to help students who struggle with _____ concept?**

These are the steps we will follow to design and answer to that question:

I. User Discovery; also called stakeholder interviews (Anticipated date of completion: June __)
This can be a one-on-one interview with the grade 10 student whose problem you are trying to solve. If multiple students identify the same area of difficulty this can be a focus group. In the event that you can't coordinate schedules, this can be done via a Form, Doc or Google Hangout.

II. Ideate: Crazy 8's (Anticipated date of completion: June __)
Ms. Whiting will visit the AP classes to guide you through an ideation (think: brainstorming) exercise and then thinking 10X by using the "Yes! And…" protocol.

III. Prototype (Anticipated date of completion: June __)
You, each of the students in both AP classes, will choose your best idea, perhaps partnering with someone solving the same or similar problem, and build a rudimentary prototype of your idea that can be tested with your stakeholder or stakeholder focus group.

I. Iteration (Anticipated date of completion: June __)
Once you have received feedback on your design, you will revise your plan and begin to build your final product.

II. Launch! (Anticipated date of completion: June __)

If all goes according to plan, you will deliver your learning support materials to the Honors classes so that the students in honors can use the materials to study for their final exam.

FIGURE 6.4 AP Chem Handout 1

USER DISCOVERY

The best way to learn about your users is to ask questions. Meet the students who identified your problem; if there are multiple people try to talk to all of them. Use this space to develop questions to ask them. It is ideal to go out and talk to the Honors Chem students, but if you can't, you could also send an email with a few questions, or send out a survey in a Google Form. Don't forget, you can Google Hangout with them as well.

USER Info: Honors Chem student (who is this person?)
Assumed Problem: What do you, the student in AP think is causing the difficulty?   **Interview Notes**: What does the student from Honors Chem tell you?
Now consider: **WHO** are you users?   **WHAT** are their needs?   **HOW** do they behave?   **WHY** do they behave that way?
Who Am I: Did I have this same problem? Am I challenged to understand why my stakeholder struggled?

CRAZY 8's Brainstorm
We will give you a large piece of blank paper -- it won't be blank for long! Fold it in half 3X, when you open it up, it will have 8 eight sections. Refer to the image to the right:

You will draw 8 different possible solutions (one in each box); for each box you will have 40 seconds to draw your idea.

There are NO bad ideas!

Think BIG! Imagine if you had access to all the information and resources that you could need.

PROTOTYPE
Following this exercise, we will think 10X by using an exercise called, "Yes! And…" to expand and improve your initial ideas, and then you will build it. The first draft will be a prototype -- enough of a product that you can test the idea on each other to be sure it will work and find places for improvement. Then, you will build the final version to deliver to the 10th grade classes.

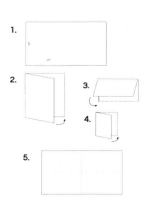

FIGURE 6.5   AP Chem Handout 2

FIGURE 6.6 AP Chem Students

At first, the students were unaccustomed to seeing me, the library media specialist, in their science class, and they quickly picked up on the trust their science teacher had in me and they followed along. Once the scope of the project was explained to them, they bought into this project right away; it tapped into their content expertise, empowered them as role models for learning, and gave them agency over the product they created. At the same time, it challenged them to suspend judgment and listen to their younger peers and not assume they knew why their peers were struggling with certain concepts. Ultimately, the AP students (Figure 6.6), in consultation with their tenth-grade peers, created exam preparation study aids that then became materials for differentiated instruction during the next school year.

CASE 4: *THE GREAT GATSBY* ESSAY

How might we explore a classic text in a way that revitalizes its impact?

Reading *The Great Gatsby*, in many high schools, continues to be a student rite of passage. Probably an English teacher's one, too! Fitzgerald's novel is a literary icon, interpreted in multiple film versions and SparkNotes. Let's face it: how many Dr. Eckleberg's glasses' essays can one teacher read? And is there anything for a student to say about them that hasn't been said already? I think not. Which makes Gatsby a fantastic opportunity for hacking with human-centered design.

I discussed the reading and teaching of Gatsby with an English teacher colleague. I asked her to describe her literary priorities for the students to explore; she said:

1. the theme of the private vs. the public;
2. Nick's unreliability as the narrator of the novel;
3. the malleable nature of memory;
4. conscious and unconscious creation of self

With these content priorities, the other consideration in hacking the reading of this novel is to maximize student ownership of the process and the ultimate project design. So let's return to the "How might we . . . ?" question stem. We have already seen how this question starter can be the gateway to diverse and powerful ways of understanding and beginning to solve a problem. By viewing the students' communication of their insights about the novel as a problem to be solved, "How might we . . ." will push them to harness their strengths and talents as creators in order to tap into the nuances of the text and its resonance across decades.

Don't believe me? Let's try to hack some traditional Gatsby essay questions with "How might we. . . ." For example, there are so many possibilities for what a student could do with the traditional literary analysis of the layers of self that Jay Gatz created. What if we pose this topic as a question such as, "How might we explain Jay Gatz's compulsion to be someone else?" A student who chooses to turn his/her focus to the narration of the novel could ask: "How might we compensate for Nick's unreliability as a narrator?" These questions necessitate that the students have agency over the question that guides their inquiry, the process they use to answer it, and the determination of what they create to demonstrate their learning.

Also important is that the question can be completed in so many ways for students to access any of the literary elements and rhetorical devices they will be studying. Consider these uses of "How might we . . .":

Amp up the good. (Doesn't Nick grow?)
Remove the bad. (We are onto Nick, so it is OK.)
Question assumptions. (Who says he is unreliable?)
Use unexpected resources. (Are there other characters offering their versions of events?)

Challenge the status quo. (It's not the narrator's job to relate to us.)
Address point of view. (Would Jordan tell the story better? Which character barely speaks, and how can we give him/her voice?)
Go after adjectives (like "unreliable"; maybe he is uninformed or naive?)
Play against the challenge. (If Fitzgerald wanted us to compensate for Nick, he would have written a different narrator.)
Explore opposites. (How might we remove the need for a narrator?)
Employ analogies. (Nick, as a narrator, is like, chocolate as a . . .)

Once students have chosen the "How might we . . ." problem they want to pursue, provide them with a selection of ideation and brainstorming tools to help them explore the possible solutions. Crazy 8s is one brainstorming example we have practiced. Following it with "Yes, And . . ." builds collaboration among the students and provides them an opportunity to be invested in each other's work, learn from each other, and practice thinking about the novel through more than one lens. Ultimately, students can work as reading and writing partners with critical peer friends and manage class discussions about the novel in which they consider the nuances of the ideas they each bring to the seminar based on the literary problem they are trying to solve. In this way, their final project—even if it is a literary analysis essay—will be quite far from the traditional papers students are usually assigned to write.

CASE 5: NINTH-GRADE WORLD HISTORY

How might we customize our presentations to meet the needs of our audience?

When we write curricula, we build it around enduring understandings and essential questions that are connected to content standards our students must master. How might we share with students the determination as to which paths through the content best enables their individual mastery? How might we empower students to design and deliver meaningful, relevant, and effective demonstrations of their learning? It was with these unit design questions in mind that I collaborated with a social studies colleague who was teaching ninth-grade World History. This particular class is entirely student centered by design and the teacher team, Drew Colati, a social studies teacher, and his coteacher who is a member of the English department, are practiced at supporting students through inquiry, self-discovery, and creative demonstrations of learning.

This is a class of fifty-five students divided into two sections. For this unit each section had to work as a unit to design, develop, and deliver their project. Here are the unit questions Drew outlined for the students:

1. What is progress? (Craft a definition of what progress means for a society.)
2. Examine the fourteenth to seventeenth centuries in Western Europe and determine if (and if so how) the Renaissance and Protestant Reformation were a time of progress.
3. Why does this matter? What drives progress? What keeps society from progressing, perfection of institutions or individual challenge of institutions?

The only other criteria that Drew gave to the class for this unit was that they could not deliver an oral presentation. Think about this for a minute. The structure of this unit was a problem with a constraint. The problem is understanding, defining, and explaining progress. The constraint: You can't stand up in front of the class and talk about it. Student-centered learning by design, for sure! Ultimately, each section of the class had to devise a way to convince the other section of their thesis without a formal debate or stand-and-deliver talk. That's where "How might we . . ." came in.

I guided the students (Figure 6.7) through a brainstorming exercise and the "Yes, And . . ." process as a strategy for them to determine the best means of conveying their argument and evidence, beginning with: how might we best convey our findings and conclusion without talking directly to the other group? Exploring this prompt required them to consider the scope of their findings and the various media they contained. It also necessitated understanding their audience and the mode or modes of delivery most likely to sustain the audience's interest and be accessible to all of them.

Let's say that one group decided that what would be most important is for the other group to hear the music, public debates, and other sounds happening

Learning by Design   71

FIGURE 6.7   Ninth-Grade Students

during these centuries. They could produce a podcast or radio show. They could create a music video by quoting and recontextualizing music and words of the era. Lots of possibilities when they start to think aurally.

Maybe the other group would decide what would be important is touch. Audiences have to hold the artifacts in their hands to understand how they worked and why they matter to the argument. In that case, the students would be very busy replicating and building hands-on items. An excellent opportunity for working in a makerspace!

Visual learning can be the students' default mode. Certainly when students were surveyed by the Pew Center in 2018 about their preferred online platforms, they reported YouTube, Instagram, and SnapChat as their top three. Today we could probably add TikTok to that list. All four are visual platforms. When studying learning styles, many students tend to self-describe as visual learners. With this learning strength and preferred content delivery medium, maybe students would decide to curate a museum exhibit using Google Arts and Culture. Or use a 360-degree camera to take a photo of a gallery scene or scenes they curate and use a program such as Google's Tour Creator to annotate the objects in the scene and render it as a virtual reality presentation. Or a living scavenger hunt where they find class members dressed in period costumes and use QR codes to provide video explanations of the scene. Given how image rich these centuries were, yet another possibility is that they might build a mosaic using many images to combine and form a dominant image that they can then annotate.

Ultimately, the students did a little bit of everything listed above and curated and organized it on websites that invited viewers to interact with the content and media that spoke to them. Recognizing that one size doesn't fit all (or even most), the students created multiple pathways through their argument just as they charted multiple pathways through their learning. Which serves to me as evidence that they are thriving in this learning environment.

What's really exciting to me is that Drew created the time and space for these students to entirely own the means by which they explored the content and by which they conveyed their learning. He challenged them by trusting them. He engaged them by trusting them. He built a learning community in his classroom in which the students know—and learn to expect—that their voices will be heard and matter. When their creative thinking and varied skill sets and experiences combine with these opportunities, the scope of their learning is boundless.

CASE 6: SIXTH-GRADE SOCIAL STUDIES

How might we reframe our understanding of human rights in order to advocate for people who are oppressed?

A huge shout-out to my friend Emma Cottier for sharing this next example of human-centered design in the classroom. Emma is a middle school teacher in British Columbia, Canada, and she is inspiring and generous with her creative ideas. Emma is a Google Certified Trainer and Innovator. We met when we both attended the Innovator Academy in Stockholm, Sweden, in 2017 and have been friends and collegial collaborators ever since. As you read about Emma's work with her students in a transdisciplinary inquiry unit, keep in mind the personas of Jay (Figure 6.12) and Antonella (Figure 6.13). I encourage you to practice gaining insight into student stakeholders by completing Figure 4.1, Understand Your Stakeholder, in order to gain insight into the needs, motivations, and interests of these two students. (I have included completed ones at the end of this section in case you want a point of comparison.) Look for points of intersection between them where they can find common ground with each other. Also, look for differences where through thoughtful collaboration they can complement each other. Finally, consider how the unit Emma designed provides students a path to mastery of her curricular goals and provides students with meaningful engagement in the content and agency over their process.

The goal of the sixth-grade Social Studies curriculum in British Columbia is to help facilitate an increased global perspective of the world. Through inquiry and instruction, students are guided to develop empathy with what daily life looks and feels like for children in other countries and to create inferences and perspectives about how people live in different places of the world.

To initiate this journey of global perspective in her classroom, sixth-grade teacher Emma Cottier introduces her students to the novel *Breadwinner* by Deborah Ellis. *Breadwinner* is the story of an eleven-year-old girl named Parvana living in Afghanistan under the Taliban rule. She lives in a one-room, bomb-stricken dwelling with her family of five. Parvana's dad was taken away for being well educated, and she is forced to dress like a boy in order to work to provide for her family. The proximity in ages between the protagonist and Emma's middle school students naturally invites the students to compare their lives and notice the significant differences in daily experiences.

The inquiry process started with the students brainstorming questions and inferences about life in Afghanistan on a graphic organizer (Figures 6.8 and 6.9). In reflecting on what she saw and heard in her class, Emma said: "Students quickly developed compassion for the main character Parvana and were able to develop powerful questions—'What is the purpose of the Taliban being in power?' or 'Why do certain groups of people fear the ability of others to be able to read and write?' The students became consumed by the story line and quickly acknowledged how other children in another country had limited rights and freedoms."

In response to the students' disbelief about the struggles Parvana faced as a result of the government systems at play where she lives, the logical next step for Emma's students was an exploration of the Universal Declaration of Human Rights (un.org/en/universal-declaration-human-rights). Their empathy for Parvana's experiences continued to grow, Emma observed, "as they discovered that all their rights and freedoms were being met on a daily basis and not a single one was being met for Parvana. Where was Parvana's voice in the daily struggle to survive? How could individuals continually turn a blind eye to the quality of life for children in these war stricken countries?"

As the student's guided inquiry continued, discussions in class turned toward a desire for action. The compassion that Emma's students were developing for children like Parvana fostered a yearning to make a difference in the lives of people being denied the fundamental human rights Emma's students realized they were taking for granted.

Adhering to principles of design, Emma recognized that her students needed the agency to create learning representations based on Parvana's story and their new understanding of life in Afghanistan that authentically conveyed their learning and the recommendation they were making for protecting the rights of children. Students were empowered to select a method that best fit their vision and would reflect their knowledge. Ultimately, Emma's sixth-grade students created powerful designs and digital displays of information. See Figures 6.10 and 6.11 as examples. Students brilliantly showcased their compassion for Parvana in a wide range of digital literacies from Instagram posts to graphic designs to newspaper articles. Emma said, "Students blew my mind with their depth of understanding and global perspective."

Name: _____
Date: _____

Double Entry Journal

Criteria:
- ☐ Quote chosen is important to the selected book or text.
- ☐ Minimum of one quote per session of reading.
- ☐ Page number is recorded beside each quote.
- ☐ Draw an image that represents your chosen quote.
- ☐ Entries show a variety of responses (Questions, Predictions, Summaries, Inferences)
- ☐ Responses explain why quote is important and/or interesting.
- ☐ Responses and quotes show effort, thought and care.

Title: _____ **Author:** _____ **Pages:** _____

Quote- Record a direct quote from your reading. Choose meaningful, thoughtful quotes. Page # _____	
Image	Record your Questions, Reactions, Important Ideas, Inferences. These need to relate directly to your quote and be in full detail.

Quote- Record a direct quote from your reading. Choose meaningful, thoughtful quotes. Page # _____	
Image	Record your Questions, Reactions, Important Ideas, Inferences. These need to relate directly to your quote and be in full detail.l

FIGURE 6.8 Parvana Organizer 1

Quote- Record a direct quote from your reading. Choose meaningful, thoughtful quotes. Page # _____

Image	Record your Questions, Reactions, Important Ideas, Inferences. These need to relate directly to your quote and be in full detail.

Quote- Record a direct quote from your reading. Choose meaningful, thoughtful quotes. Page # _____

Image	Record your Questions, Reactions, Important Ideas, Inferences. These need to relate directly to your quote and be in full detail.

Quote- Record a direct quote from your reading. Choose meaningful, thoughtful quotes. Page # _____

Image	Record your Questions, Reactions, Important Ideas, Inferences. These need to relate directly to your quote and be in full detail.

FIGURE 6.9 Parvana Organizer 2

Learning by Design 77

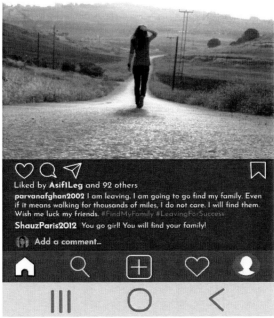

FIGURE 6.10 Parvana Instagram

In just a few short weeks students were engaged and captivated in a world completely different from their own. They connected to the protagonist Parvana living in Afghanistan in heartfelt ways and explored complex global issues that contribute to unfortunate living situations for children around the world. Because Emma's goal was to foster her students' empathy with Parvana and children like her (rather than judgment or sympathy), their projects were not directives for what Parvana or her family should do differently. Instead, they designed actions that we are invited to take together to do our part to ensure that human rights are protected for everyone and to not be content if our rights are secure when someone else's are not. "Their journey focused on the life of a human being," Emma commented, "and I have no doubt that this journey through Afghanistan will leave a lasting impact on how they view the world and how they seek solutions to global issues."

78 Student-Centered Learning by Design

FIGURE 6.11 Parvana News

You might have noticed from the projects that Emma's students created that they are quite adept at rendering visuals digitally. Emma is a master of Google Draw and makes powerful use of it as a learning tool. I encourage you to check out more of her work with her students. To continue learning with Emma, you can follow her on Twitter @EmmaCottier.

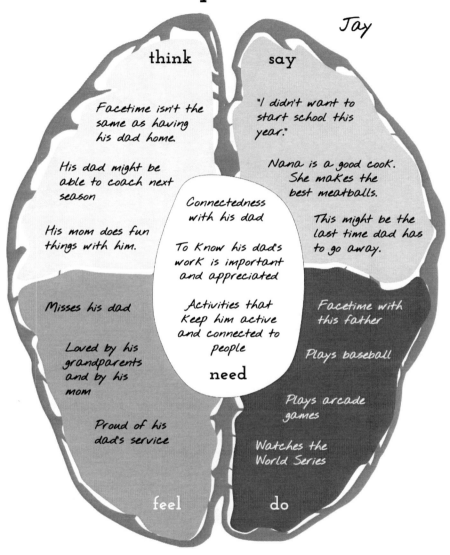

FIGURE 6.12 Student (Jay) Completed

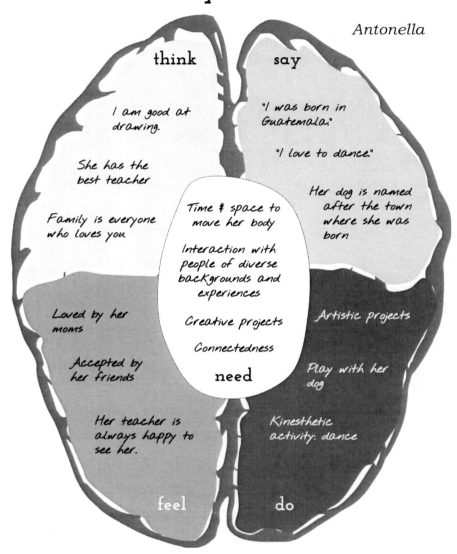

FIGURE 6.13 Student (Antonella) Completed

CASE 7: CAREER AND TECHNICAL EDUCATION (CTE) AND DESIGN

How might we coax students to struggle?

When you hear mention of "tech ed," what comes to mind? I think many of us think coding, computational thinking, AP computer science classes, and the like. While that is all part of it, let's broaden that lens and remember that the roots of CTE (career and technical education) are in what used to be known as Industrial Arts classes. When I was in middle school, I took woodshop and metal shop, cooking and sewing classes. My high school had a full auto mechanics garage and offered auto shop classes. I graduated from high school in 1986, just as these programs were beginning to wane. According to University of Michigan professor and former Brookings expert Brian A. Jacobs, "Starting in the 1980s, states increased the number of courses required for high school graduation, and began mandating students take additional courses in core academic areas such as math, science, social studies and foreign language. These additional requirements, along with declining funding and a growing perception that all young people should be encouraged to obtain a four-year college degree, led to a sharp decline in CTE participation. Between 1990 and 2009, the number of CTE credits earned by U.S. high school students dropped by 14 percent."

While these classes have fallen victim to budget cuts, the Fourth Industrial Revolution has refocused education attention on STEM, STEAM, and STREAM; on maker spaces and learning commons; all of which have their roots in the hands-on tinkering of the applied arts. Think of today's maker movement as STEM: OG. In this context I would like to introduce you to Ashley O'Connor, a CTE teacher at a public high school in Connecticut. For a short time, Ashely and I were colleagues at the same high school and collaborated on projects with her game design and web design classes. This is just a small sampling of Ashely's tech ed skill set. She also teaches a DIY class that includes plumbing and electrical work, an automotive maintenance class, woodshop, engineering drafting, and architecture. Needless to say, design is the basis of everything Ashley does, whether it is working with her students in these classes or building custom-stained glass cabinet doors for her kitchen.

Ashley said that she and her CTE colleagues struggle with an essential design question: "How might we get students to try?" On the one hand, that seems so basic, and on the other hand, it resonates with teachers in many different disciplines. What distinguishes her department from others is that "students aren't coming into our classes with any background knowledge." Ashley remembered how her dad taught her to take care of her car maintenance and be not just comfortable but skilled with his collection of power tools. "Baby boomers were taught this stuff at home," Ashley commented. "Now there is a skills gap. Other tech has evolved and people stopped doing their own home maintenance or they stopped having their kids help."

Why is this a problem to be solved? As Ashley describes it, "These are life skills. People don't realize that tech is utilizing every subject area to create an outcome and acceptance of risk is essential to learning here. Every day we fight against our students' fear of trying." And every day, the students in

Ashley's classes are solving problems. In DIY, the easiest problem they solve is unclogging and repairing a toilet. The students go on a scavenger hunt through the lab trying to secure the tools they will need; they are equipped with permission to try anything they think will work and any tutorials they can find to guide them. The hardest part for the teachers, Ashley says, is to resist stepping in and giving answers. Eventually, the students realize that Ashley will respond to their questions and solicitations of the "right" solution with more questions, and they begin to work with each other to figure it out. "I just keep reminding them that all of the resources they need are in the classroom tangibly or digitally and that they have a brain, a way to figure out the answers." And eventually the toilets are restored to working order.

She wishes every student took these classes. In automotive class, each student does a close examination of the car they drive regularly or the car in which they are most frequently a passenger. They read the manual, and they know how to find the corresponding digital version online. Auto shops aren't just for vocational schools. "It's about maintenance and car safety." Ashely said. When her school was undergoing a renovation, Ashley invited the project manager to visit her classes and discuss his perspective on CTE curricula. Her students were amazed to hear him discuss his dismay at having to teach the adults he employs some of what he considers to be the basic skills of their jobs: problem solving, flexible thinking, collaboration, etc.—which underscored the importance of the courses in which they are enrolled.

One of her frustrations working with her students is that they do not research well. Librarians who are used to having social studies teachers as their primary collaboration partners for teaching research and inquiry, might find all new partnerships can be forged with their CTE colleagues. "The students don't take what they are learning in their other classes and transfer it to our field," Ashley commented. "And if they are going to solve problems, like building a model home that meets Habitat for Humanity criteria including ADA compliance and green construction, they need inquiry skills." This project is part of the Connecticut Home Show annual competition. While the students are designing a dream house according to their own aesthetic, without a thorough understanding of the needs of the different people who might live in their home and the practices and resources available for green construction, the students' designs and prototypes fall short of meeting the purposes of the design challenge. When Ashley says that tech ed includes the skills of all of the other disciplines, she is not exaggerating. Question formulation and research; measuring, calculating, and quantifying; communicating and collaborating; delivery of an aesthetically satisfying and functional prototype. As Ashley was describing this project and the metacognitive processes her students were using and their commitment to the project, and the portfolios they built, I couldn't help but think about the portrait of the graduate and the purposeful way in which these students are demonstrating skill and content mastery by synthesizing their learning to problem solve for their community. What an incredible example. Ashley's students' work is for a collaborative team of educators, including the librarian, to use when building curricula and problem-based learning experiences.

You can follow Ashley on Twitter @techedteachAO to see the amazing work she and her students are doing.

CASE 8: RETHINKING THE TRADITIONAL PUBLIC POLICY PAPER IN CIVICS CLASS

How might we advocate for public policy to address problems we experience in the United States?

For this unit, I collaborated with a social studies teacher, Meredith Ramsey, in her civics classes. We used the design thinking process to hack a traditional assessment—the public policy research paper—and turned the new public policy project into a human-centered design inquiry experience for her students. The intention of the original public policy paper was that it be grounded in the students' interests, be research based, and culminate in formal writing. The challenges posed by the old paradigm were that students ended up—despite the best intentions and ongoing intervention by the teachers—writing reports without a problem-solving mindset. The final papers were devoid of any action that the students, themselves, would or could take, and, as a result, the students didn't buy into early lessons on important research skills.

So, Meredith reframed this unit as the public policy project: the students were going to solve problems. We began with the question: "How might we advocate for public policy to address problems we experience in the United States?" To do this required the students' investment in their problems, focused and thorough research, commitment to actionable solutions, and the ability to convincingly communicate their findings.

Students tackled issues including:

The opioid crisis
Tobacco and e-cigarette advertising
Climate change
Health care access
Gun violence
Domestic violence
Pollution
Data privacy
Student athlete exploitation

Meredith explains that the "we" part of the "How might we . . ." question is what hooked her: the work the students would be doing for this project would be collaborative, authentically so. Beyond that, the governing philosophy to the civics class that she teaches is that government and citizenship are active, not passive. A course outcome is for the students to develop a sense of agency and understanding of their capacity to take informed action. Sample student HMW question: How might we instill regulations on the use of CRISPR (clustered regularly interspaced short palindromic repeats) technology in order to allow for medical advancements to be made while ensuring that the welfare of the patient is put first?

Another big win for Meredith was the quality of the collaboration in which her students engaged. After the initial stage of researching to validate the scope of the problem they were addressing and to gain insight into the impact of the problem on the people who experience it, each student shared his/her/their research organizer with another student in the class for feedback. The class used "The Five Whys" protocol to create a peer-to-peer feedback loop that proved valuable to helping each student assess how well they truly understood the problem they were researching and the stakeholders. (See Figure 6.14, Digging into the Problem Organizer.) Here's how it worked:

Partner A shared the research organizer (in Google Doc form) with Partner B. Partner B read it and found one place to ask a "Why?" question. Partner A responded to that question—and in many cases, Partner A provided URLs to sources to justify the response. Partner B read the response and asked another "Why?" question. Partner A responded, and so on, until B had asked five "Why?" questions. This process helped make the students' thinking visible to Meredith so she could provide focused and purposeful feedback and direction and prompted meaningful reflection by the students on both the substance of their research and their understanding of the stakeholders.

Ultimately, the project succeeded beyond Meredith's expectations. "Throughout the process, students' thinking was visible which made it easier for me and for the students to evaluate the work that was being done." Because the students kept their problem at the heart of their project, they were committed to being able to take action; the students learned how to think differently about themselves and the value of what they were learning. And, icing on the cake, Meredith said, "this experience has increased my confidence as a teacher."

Digging into the Problem

What is the problem?	
Who is affected by this problem? How many people? How old are they? What are their current behaviors? Where do they live? Who might be impacted by the potential solutions?	**When did this problem start and what might happen if nothing is done about it?**
Why does this problem concern you? Why should other people be concerned about this problem?	
Source Citations	

FIGURE 6.14 Digging into the Problem Organizer

CASE 9: DESIGNING FOR A MULTIGRADE CLASSROOM

How might we shift students from passive recipients of content to active participants in their learning?

Arianna Lambert is an elementary school teacher in Toronto, Canada. She also happens to be a brilliant practitioner of human-centered design in the classroom. Her journey as an educator epitomizes what it means to embrace design thinking as a mindset rather than a process. As you read Arianna's story, keep in mind the persona of third-grade student Jocelyn and the habits of mind (i.e., learned behaviors of compliance) that she is beginning to internalize.

In her class this year Arianna has five fifth-grade students and sixteen fourth-grade students. Reflecting on the grouping of students in her class and their habits of mind around grades, Arianna noted, "It has been an interesting year with my students looking for right answers with a tell-me-what-you-want-me-to-say mindset. At the start of the year they just didn't realize that the mark isn't the end all be all. They need to see that learning is a process." To that end, even with students as young as fourth grade, Arianna confronts the compliance challenge: tell me what I need to do to get the grade I want and I will do it. "I want my students to learn that I am not looking for them to agree with me about everything—it's OK to disagree with me, do it politely, and argue your point. Good grades aren't about compliance and compliance isn't self-regulation. I want students to be able to acknowledge when they don't understand something, and say, 'help me figure this out; why are we doing this again?'" Arianna admitted, "When they ask why it helps me keep it in perspective—why AM I asking you to do this. I want them to keep asking why?" Students who learn to question the world around them whether out of curiosity or concern can then develop confidence in their capacity to be positive agents of change.

The problem-solving mindset that Arianna is nurturing in her students is the same optimistic point of view she brings to planning for her very heterogeneous class. "Design is the way to meet the needs of diverse groups of learners—if we always begin by focusing on empathy and solving problems we can apply that anywhere, to any discipline. And students build skills and ways of thinking. 'This is a problem; let's see how we can solve it' is a good mindset to have." In some instances Arianna can provide instruction with all of the students together while differentiating for their levels. In math, for example, Arianna said, "I start with what the fours need and assure that the grade fives already know it, and then I enrich for grade four when teaching the content for grade five. So the fours are exposed to the grade five content, but I don't assess grade fours on it." Whoa! Here's a content example of how that works: fourth grade studies perimeter and area; these dimensions are the foundations for volume, which is the content for the fifth grade. The application of this learning takes the form of a whole class design challenge: build a safe playscape for the kindergartners.

This problem-solving project began with a KWC exercise: What do we know? What do we want to know? What are our conditions? (think: design constraints.)

The fourth and fifth graders together had to examine the existing lot and identify safety and equipment issues from the lack of a fence in a neighborhood where lots of people walk by to the need for some play equipment to be replaced. Arianna's students interviewed the kindergarteners to understand how they liked to play and what their favorite outdoor activities were. They were developing empathy with the primary users of the space they were designing. Then, the fourth and fifth graders had to research construction materials to learn what was available from the approved vendor and what fit the principal's budget. They used Google Maps to measure the different dimensions they needed and compared prices to decide which materials were most cost effective for meeting their users' needs. They discussed and made decisions regarding how much of the budget to put toward new play equipment and how much they would recycle and reuse. When they learned that some of the little students like scooters and others like to climb things, the fourth and fifth graders wrestled with the question: how might we meet all of their recreational needs and stay within budget? "They worked to solve a real problem that we live with." Arianna said. "In the big problem they see the purpose of the math we are studying. They bring lots of ideas to the table."

In other content areas, in particular for science and social studies, Arianna designs learning sessions for which she breaks the class into grade-level groups because the content for each grade level is entirely different. Yet, the students can still come together for interdisciplinary design projects. By engaging the students in these collaborative, authentic problem-solving challenges, she is helping the students to unlearn compliance and let go of the extrinsic grade-based measure of achievement. Her students are starting to understand that learning is ongoing, that they, as problem solvers, continue to grow and evolve. When the fifth-grade students were studying how forces work on structures, Arianna challenged them to design and build a bridge. "The students had examined lots of information about bridges, how they are built and what forces they withstand. When it came time to test their bridges, every group failed epically: some because the bridge couldn't withstand the weight placed on it, others because there was too much tension, and so the students started talking about how and why the bridges failed." Arianna directed them to improve their designs. She told them, "You know what to do, so make them better. Tell me when you're ready to test them again." That's what she said instead of giving them a deadline. She gave them agency over the design, the iteration, and process. "They are struggling with it." She admitted. It is a good struggle.

CASE 10: BUILDING A SAFE LEARNING ENVIRONMENT IN THIRD GRADE

How might we eliminate bullying in our classroom?

Sometimes the stakeholder for a design project can be the very class that is embarking on the design journey. Rachel Swanson, the director of academics for the Lutheran schools in Chicago and the founder of Rachel Swanson Coaching, shared with me the story of one of her classes back when she was a third-grade teacher. In fact, when I explained that I wanted her to share a story about using human-centered design with her elementary students, she immediately exclaimed, "Oh! I know exactly the story I want to share!"

Rachel taught multiple elementary grade levels on the south side of Chicago in a neighborhood that had high rates of poverty, and project-based learning had long been the bedrock of Rachel's pedagogy. Of all the grades she taught, third grade is the one she taught the most. "I had one particular class that was absolutely delightful," Rachel remembered. One of the projects Rachel facilitated for this class was when they were studying their water unit in science, the class turned the classroom into an underwater ecosphere. She is absolutely one of the most creative and patient educators I have met.

Another tenet to Rachel's pedagogy is the development of a safe learning environment. "I worked a ton with my students on building community and conflict resolution skills. I feel strongly about fostering social-emotional learning skills (SEL), and just like every teacher, there would be kids in my classroom who had behavioral issues in my class. It was important to me to work with the students to understand that the role of the community was to support everyone's needs." Because the students trusted Rachel and believed in their capacity to resolve issues that affected their learning community, they were comfortable bringing forth issues to be addressed. "A group of students in the class came to me because they were concerned about bullying that was happening between students in the class. So we called an emergency class meeting."

Everyday Rachel's class held a meeting. The day after the students came to Rachel, she called an additional emergency class meeting. The urgency of this meeting showed the students how seriously Rachel was taking their concerns. She shifted what the class was going to discuss that day and, instead, they talked about how the bullying was an issue. In preparation for this initial discussion of what the class could do about the problem, Rachel went to the library and checked out every book on bullying she could find. Computers and digital resources were scarce in this school, so Rachel bought materials to bring to class to supplement what the library could provide. The students read the books and talked through how both the bullying episodes and what they were reading about made them feel. "We really worked on the empathy piece to start. Then using what they learned we started to brainstorm. We started with the "bad idea factory," and the kids came up with as many ideas as they could about what we could do about the bullying." Then Rachel asked her students to vote on which ideas they wanted to develop. "Some ideas stayed on the idea board and others were worked on," Rachel said.

During reading time the students continued to study the issue by reading articles and books to further inform their problem solving. During social studies and science time they worked on prototyping and building their plans. In the end, the class designed several different solutions to the problem and expanded the scope of their advocacy beyond Rachel's classroom and into the whole school.

The first thing they did was make bully tickets. "Like traffic tickets," Rachel described. "If a student saw someone get bullied or if a student was the target of bullying behavior, the student could fill out a ticket with checkboxes about the behaviors. Everyone in class was on board for it—everyone could fill it out." Then, on Friday, Rachel and the class would review the tickets to see what issues could be resolved by the students on their own and which needed intervention. "We had really deep discussions." Rachel remembered. "If someone had a lot of tickets that student had the opportunity to ask the class for support and help with ways they could change what they were doing. When one kid said that he was lonely, the other students committed to sitting with him at lunch. Another kid told us that he got angry a lot. The other kids helped him think of strategies for when he felt that way. The classmates also learned that sometimes they just had to leave him alone when he said he was angry."

In all honesty, I was blown away listening to Rachel describe this experience. This solution was designed by the students to help themselves and each other. They practiced empathy, empowered their voices, and they developed emotional intelligence. "The kids had better answers than what I could come up with!" Rachel acknowledged. "If I had tried to solve the bullying problem alone, my solution would not have been as good. This had their voice, their input, their signature all over it. They made it happen and followed through on it."

Other students expanded the work of the class and created an antibullying poster campaign for the school and spoke to their peers to raise their awareness at the weekly school assembly. Another group of students became interested in cyberbullying and did research on their own outside of school and presented to class about what it is, how to prevent it, and how to stay safe on the Internet, all with their peers as an authentic audience.

"We so often are reactive to situations in our classrooms with discipline referral slips when the solutions to problems can live in our own classrooms, with the students who are experiencing the situations." This observation invites an exploration of two more personas: Mitch, the school counselor, and Gloria, the administrator. Imagine a partnership between these faculty members and a teacher like Rachel with a problem like the one her students presented and students who have learned, through the building of classroom culture, to be actively engaged as problem solvers in their community. When we examine our school's climate and research ways to incorporate social-emotional learning into our day-to-day routines, we frequently wrestle with how to authentically provide all members of the community with agency in decision making, and empowerment to be positive agents of change. Rachel had twenty-five students in her class that year, and they turned into twenty-five problem-solving allies and self-helpers. That is an empowering experience they will carry with them.

Rachel is a powerhouse educator. I encourage you to follow her teaching and coaching on Twitter (@racheldswanson) and check out her website at www.rachelswansoncoaching.com.

CASE 11: AN ENTREPRENEURIAL EDUCATOR PROMOTING STUDENT AGENCY

How might we empower kids to self-advocate for their learning needs?

Jennifer De Lisi-Hall is a passionate educator. In 2018 she received an Educator of Excellence award from the New York State English Council, and while she is an extraordinary teacher of English at both the middle and high school levels, she is also an experienced and accomplished instructional coach and student advocate. She is a third-generation educator, so you might say that student-centered learning is hardwired into her DNA. Her deep dive into design thinking led her down an entrepreneurial path on which she had not anticipated she would embark, yet now, it seems a logical intersection of her talents as an educator, her experience as the parent of a neurodiverse learner, and her creative problem-solving capacity.

For the last year, Jen has been designing and overseeing the building of an educational app to help not just neurodiverse learners, but ultimately all learners track and assess the effectiveness of their learning strategies, including any accommodations and modifications they have been assigned. "This is a passion project, a labor of love." Jen told me. "While it certainly is entrepreneurial, I'm doing it based on my motivations. This is my twentieth year teaching, special ed is where my heart is, this is where I live personally and professionally. I want to see this tool in wide use to help kids, not to make money."

Before you continue reading about Jen's project development process and about how the app works, pause for a moment and conjure a student you know who has a 504 plan or special education individualized education program (IEP). Instead of using a supplied persona, this time you are proceeding with a real student whom you know in mind. Maybe you bring to mind a student you have had in class or maybe the student who comes to mind is your child. Complete the "Understand Your Stakeholder" (Figure 4.1) exercise for this student. You might want to continue digging into your stakeholder by drafting a problem statement, identifying resources and insights for that stakeholder, and even building a "How might we . . ." question that you can compare with the ultimate question Jen used.

OK. Back to Jen.

In November 2018, Jen attended a Google Innovator Academy in Copenhagen, Denmark. When applying to the Academy, prospective innovators must present a problem in education that they are committed to working to solve. When describing her experience at the Academy, Jen said, "I came to Innovator with a different problem and pivoted because this new problem is where my heart is. Solving this problem will be harder but there is more heart behind it." After returning from the Academy, Jen's project has taken on a life of its own and become the app, TurnSignal.

She started with teachers in mind as her stakeholders and asked, "How might we help teachers balance the diverse needs of kids in their classrooms to promote equity and accessibility?" As she continued researching her problem and interviewing teachers, she realized that an individual teacher might have more than a hundred students and be highly motivated to meet all of those students' learning needs. The question is how to keep it all straight? That's when collaboration with a colleague (remember: collaboration is essential to the design process) led to an epiphany: the student is the learner, the learning needs are (and will always be) the student's. Maybe, thought Jen, my stakeholders are the kids! And she switched her focus.

Instead of making it easier for teachers to organize accommodations, she asked herself, what if we empower kids and give them voice and agency to know more about their accommodations so they can self-advocate and provide feedback on how well their learning plans are working for them? And so, her design question became: how might we empower kids to self-advocate for their learning needs?

These changes and the current path of the app's development are in response to the stories kids are telling her, their stories of their accommodations. Describing the Planning and Placement Team (PPT) process, Jen said: "We meet once a year to go over IEPs [Individualized Education Programs] and 504 plans and we very rarely ask kids about their experience with accommodations except in those meetings. This is the problem. When we do ask, we say, 'how well is it working for you,' and the students smile and nod. Even a kid with great executive functioning can be intimidated by a room of adults so they aren't really expressing their needs. These are the stories I got from kids and what I saw when I attended these meetings. What came across universally, is that kids would benefit from knowing more about what their accommodations are supposed to do for them." They need a way to signal, on a regular basis, what is working for them and what is not.

Jen collected this information through conversations with students across a wide spectrum of grade levels, and what she heard resonated with her experiences as both an educator and a parent. So she started to design a way for students to record when they were using different learning strategies, accommodations, or modifications and comment on whether and how their learning was positively affected by it. Her first prototype was simply a Google Sheet for collecting feedback from students. Eventually, she hired a developer who created an MVP (minimum viable product) that she could distribute to small circles of potential users in order to beta test the concept and give her feedback.

At the time of our interview, Jen's research and development was at a point where she had enough feedback that she was planning a second phase of crowdfunding in order to finance the building of the first full version of the app, now called TurnSignal. Through the app development process Jen has been a designer and a learner, attending lots of events for start-ups and small business owners, networking with people in the edtech field, and researching funding and development models. One of her big takeaways: "Nothing has gone according to the timeline yet." Jen said that there have already been many iterations and a lot of mistakes. For example, in one of the earlier versions, the student interface began with the accommodation. "Because I was thinking about it as a teacher would. I am focused on the accommodation, but that isn't how kids see their day." Jen said, "And that point of entry was not helpful to a kid." Now it has been redesigned—which is an expensive proposition when working with an app developer—so that the student starts with the subject or class and then considers which accommodations he/she/they are using and whether they are working. It has also been streamlined for fewest possible clicks

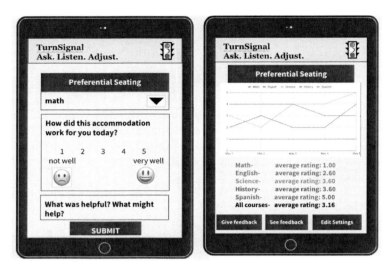

FIGURE 6.15 TurnSignal Mock-Up

so that using the app to collect real-time data about the use and effectiveness of different learning strategies doesn't occupy too much of their time.

After each class the student will input how well a learning strategy worked. They will use a Leichert sliding scale with emojis for younger users and have a place for entering comments. Then the app charts the feedback and provides an average to see that in math, for example, a copy of class notes is working well but not so well in English. Now the teacher team can brainstorm how to leverage what works in math to help English or see a strategy that works well across morning classes is less effective in the afternoon. Jen described how the reviews collected by the app will benefit students, teachers, and parents: "As we build it out, the app will alert the adult who is attached to the account to see that the student has rated a particular learning strategy, say, a 3 out of 5 for 3 days in a row . . . that is the turn signal—it indicates to the adults that a lane change is necessary. And it puts the student in the driver's seat. Kids are in control of reviewing their accommodations and giving real-time feedback. What is learned from that feedback becomes actionable to the adults—the parents and the teachers—and empowers the students to have a voice in their annual meetings."

Working within the constraints of data privacy, Jen shifted the app again, this time toward parents as primary users. "It's easier to enroll the parents first, and then sign up their student, because the user is ultimately a kid." So now Jen is focusing on parents to get it into kids' hands and is collecting input from parents as stakeholders. What she found from speaking to parents is that "they want to be part of their kids' experience in a good way. Parents want to understand and help the accommodations be more carefully chosen and to know there is effectiveness."

Jen and I share a timeline goal. By the time you are reading this book, her full app will be out of testing and ready for deployment! You can look for it here (http://turnsignal.app), and you can follow Jen and the evolution of TurnSignal on Twitter and Instagram: @Jaydel818 and @TurnSignalApp.

CASE 12: SOLVING REAL-WORLD PROBLEMS THROUGH GAME-BASED DESIGN

How might we engage learners of any age in real-world problem solving?

This is a case study in the value of feedback well received and thoughtfully implemented. It is a quintessential example of how to iterate on an idea and turn a concept into a scalable product. Before you dive into this case study, I encourage you to check out Solve in Time at https://solveintime.com. This game, created by Dee Lanier, combines the collaborative and motivational attributes of game-based learning with the empathy and authentic problem-solving elements of design. It is a powerful tool for introducing design into any content and infusing any curriculum with real-world problem solving. Part of the beauty of Solve in Time (#SolveIT) is the simplicity of the tools: in its current iteration, it is simply a deck of cards with questions to guide student inquiry. The stages of problem solving unfold, inviting students to engage with one another to pool their resources and perspectives and design a solution. As learners gain understanding and insight and grow personally, the game experience matches their development, which makes it as useful with adults as with elementary students.

In both his undergraduate and graduate studies Dee majored in sociology with concentrations in race relations and education and entered the profession of education as a lateral-entry teacher. "As I learned, I applied what made sense; learning as I grew." Solve in Time is the product of that very mindset! His first six years teaching were at an alternative high school for students who were not succeeding in a traditional high school setting. In that learning community he continued to deconstruct ideas and pedagogy. "I kept asking: how can we make this work because I know it is not connecting with my kids. My mission was to connect with my kids." You will see that connecting with learners in real and authentic ways is a theme that pervades all that Dee does.

Dee's journey as an educator and his process creating Solve in Time exemplify the potency of a design thinking mindset and the unmeasurable benefits of human-centered design as pedagogy. His introduction to design came through a certified STEM program offered by Discovery Place (the science and technology museum in Charlotte, North Carolina). "What was so cool and unique about that program is that participants were forced to get approval from the schools where they teach to secure time off for intense PD every Friday to become a STEM fellow. That was the first time as an education practitioner that I participated in an experience that really valued hands-on learning that was very much differentiated and collaborative—all things I strove to do as a teacher."

This intensive professional development program is a model for the kinds of learning experiences that nurture students to collaborate, think critically, and problem solve. Dee and the other STEM fellows were presented with a series of different challenges building on one another, layering high-level math with science, which Dee confessed triggered his "personal sense of inadequacy, frustration and fears of being exposed as not being great at math." He laughed, saying that like students, teachers are good at different things, and success results from working as a team. At one point during the program, "a box of stuff came out and they said we want you to figure out how to build a motor and have the pencil move from this side of the line to the other." Dee was practically giddy remembering this challenge. "I said move out of the way y'all—feeling complete empowerment and excitement. I know I'm good at this—just being a tinkerer that gave me that confidence."

Many of us have those serendipitous encounters with people whose mentorship and influence helped steer the path we have traveled. One of the program leads at Discovery Place filled this role for Dee. "We had long philosophical conversations about design thinking and what we called human-centered learning. We talked about museum programs that were total failures and asked ourselves why is it a failure? Why aren't people interacting with that installation? We discussed how users will do what is most intuitive so signs and directions don't really matter." Understanding people's motivation and behavior is the basis of design. The lessons from these conversations manifest themselves in a design decision when Dee created Solve in Time. "I don't give a ton of directions—bulk instructions confuse and frustrate me. I read them slowly and outloud. Now I am experienced enough to know I am not less of a learner. Growing up I did think that." That self-awareness results in Dee's relentless work to make Solve in Time as universally accessible and valuable as possible.

In 2016, Dee was accepted into the Google Innovator Academy where one of the coaches handed him a copy of *Design Thinking for Educators* and told him "You should have this book. You are going to do great things." After which Dee said, "Design thinking was something that just integrated into what I was doing." What he was doing was building an early iteration of Solve in Time called SmashboardEDU.

"I want to have kids get their hands on stuff and learn that way," offered Dee. He was working on two projects at the time: Maker Kitchen—Dee is a fan of low-cost, blended-learning making—and SmashboardEDU, a game he had started developing with his students. "It began as a gamified version of hyperdocs. I saw problematic things in hyperdocs and began making it more fun." The intent was for the learning in SmashboardEDU to still be guided by the teacher and paced by the students. SmashboardEDU blended a game-board design and app smashing, and Dee's students loved it. "I learned," Dee reflected, "the more I implemented design thinking as part of the process, the more I started to recognize the things that were problematic. App-smashing [creating a product through the use of multiple content creation apps, a product that cannot be created by one app alone] became the goal, and I wanted students to solve real world problems. My goal was helping students connect to social justice problems and the people involved with those problems in order to begin working on solutions to those problems."

A real-world problem faced by parents in Dee's community actually informed an iteration of the game. Traditionally, Martin Luther King Jr. Day was a school holiday until the year that Dee's home state of North Carolina had so many snow days that school was held on that holiday. "A friend told me: my kid came home today and told me so much about MLK that I didn't know historically. So kids went to school today and learned so much stuff I couldn't teach them at home." Which prompted Dee to wonder, "What if we could create something that could be an at-home activity parents could play with their kids." The contexts in which the game can be meaningfully experienced continued to grow.

Here is where the value of openness to feedback is apparent. Some colleagues started pointing out that once kids got into the process of working with the apps, even if they created something cool, their energy was being invested in app-based creation rather than the substance of the problem they were solving. "Then," Dee said, "the kids pointed it out, and I started to listen. It became my thing with my students. I'm going to ask for feedback every day and we are going to iterate this until it gets really really good." Dee started presenting it at conferences, which is when he recognized a gap between how students and adults learn: "Students are more inclined to fill in a gap in instructions. If I don't say how to get from A to C students will figure out B. Teachers get frustrated quickly without B. If I wanted to transform teaching and learning, teachers had to be on board." Dee's takeaway: Understanding how to play the game shouldn't be the hard part—that energy should be channeled into solving the problem. Thus the game, now rebranded as Solve in Time, became a series of design questions that help guide the learner through a problem-solving process. All of those educators and conference session attendees "didn't realize how much they were helping me to make it better by expressing their frustration!" Dee asserted.

Dee explained another design change happened because "I always wanted to make it a physical game. I envisioned a game board. I had cards, spinners, dice—there were so many different mediums that I experimented with"—it turned into cards when students told him that sometimes playing with the dice became a distraction from dealing with the problem. Dice out, cards in! His students were his prototype beta testers, sometimes creating a product that was a solution to a problem, sometimes evaluating the game process itself, all the while internalizing the mindset of designers themselves.

When Dee learned hermeneutics from a campus ministry, question asking became a critical component to the game. "How do you properly understand a text that is written for one audience and then is applied in a new context? Who, what, when, where, why questions. You have to answer these before you do anything else. You can't properly interpret what's going on unless you first properly understand what's going on. And you can't properly apply your learning unless you have a good interpretation." That is how Solve in Time became question driven, and as a result, one of the potent features of Solve in Time is that it is so responsive to sociopolitical issues—check out the SEL and antiracism expansion packs—and adaptable to any educational needs.

I asked Dee why he offers so much of the game downloadable for free. His answer: "because so much of it was given to me. It was my vision and desire to make something happen, but I can't even name the people who all gave feedback and that collective effort is what makes it successful." From session attendees who shared their frustrations and some who sat and talked with Dee about it to his former students and his own kids and friends all of whom gave tons of support, "this is a community-built project." Dee said. He went on to say that it is also "an equity issue for me. I want people to play it and solve real world problems. I do what I can to make that happen. Hours upon hours, upon days and months is invested in producing it and getting it to where it is. It is not a non-profit, though I use a non-profit reinvestment model approach. All investment feeds back to create better systems, more projects, and to give swag to educators who use it."

Solve in Time is truly a passion project. "The more you get people who believe in you, you begin to think maybe I can do more, maybe I shouldn't give it up. At every point when I felt like quitting, I would get a reachout from someone saying: hey, could you do a presentation on Solve in Time? We think it is amazing! And so the design and creation process is sustained."

You can follow Dee at @deelanier and @solveintime.

Notes

This is a passion project, a labor of love... special ed is where my heart is... I want to see this tool in wide use to help kids, not to make money.

7

Distance Learning by Design

Considered holistically, I think there is an important, universal element evident in the case studies: when learning is student centered by design, the students become flexible, agile, and self-directed learners. While much necessary attention has been paid to the needs, deficits, and inequities exposed by the recent pandemic and resulting school closures, it is important also to note that some students flourished. So did some educators. The closing of schools with little advance notice or opportunity to prepare curricularly, pedagogically, or social-emotionally was traumatizing and forced schools and families into triage mode. Much of the initial professional development attention, resources, and energy was directed to building educators' technological proficiency—whether that meant learning how to maintain a learning management platform, virtual class meeting, or any other digital form of communication and interaction. As weeks wore on and comfort levels with these tools increased, attention refocused on the pedagogy of distance learning. Some educators started to wonder: How might we build community connections and sustain relationships despite our geographical distancing? How might we empower our students to demonstrate mastery in unique ways? How might we leverage all of these digital tools to provide students multiple pathways to both learn and demonstrate their learning?

A willingness to take risks is a habit of mind we want to foster in our students. Acknowledging that learning is borne not out of success but of failure, reflection, and persistence, we challenge our students to stretch out of their comfort zones. One thing is for sure, the closing of schools across the globe catapulted educators, students, and families out of their comfort zones. We weren't just talking about risk-taking; we were forced to do it, daily, and for weeks on end. In so many ways we failed—families didn't have enough (or any) devices or connectivity; we tried to use a tool at the exact moment that every other teacher in the world tried to use it so it crashed; try as we might, we just couldn't get our screen to share; and despite our best time management and planning, the dog (or child or spouse) insisted on our attention in the middle of virtual class. And the educational world didn't end. People stepped up with mobile hotspots and donated devices, we learned and tried yet other tools while edtech companies expanded capacity and functionality of their platforms to meet the demand, we finally clicked the right icon and our screen projected, and we learned to prioritize our mental wellness and helped others do the same. We researched, collaborated, prototyped, tested, pivoted, and iterated as necessary. We embraced our inner designers.

We also let go of all of the things we couldn't control. As we realized that many elements of in-person school did not have a direct digital corollary, we started to think creatively about learning scenarios. Many schools began remote teaching by requiring students to have the same hours of seat time (now in front of their computer screens) that they had when schools were open. It didn't take some of those schools long to abandon that plan and rethink what it means to empower students to learn when and how they are able. Doing so meant giving up control—frankly, it was only an illusion of control at that point anyway—and embracing UDL (Universal Design for Learning) pedagogy in order for students to be engaged, chart their own path through carefully curated learning resources, and become content creators who could share their demonstrations of learning with a wide audience.

Essentially, as the dust settled, an educational constant became clear: the elements of good teaching hadn't changed. Despite the lack of shared geographical space and the altered patterns of the day, deep learning happened when:

- a potent hook was used to **engage** students' interest;
- self-directed topic **exploration** was encouraged;
- teachers provided direct **explanation** and instruction via multiple pathways;
- students had opportunities to **apply** their learning in content creation;
- students could **share** their insight;
- guidance was provided to help students **reflect** on their learning process; and
- for those interested, opportunities to **extend** their learning for further enrichment were made possible.

See bit.ly/SCplanning for a copy of Figure 7.1, Student-Centered Planning, a template that maps out these principles for unit planning purposes.

	Before Unit Implementation		Upon Unit Completion
	What will the students do? (curiosity, agency, risk-taking, collaboration)	How will I know it worked? (gather formative and summative evidence)	Did it work? (what modifications are necessary?)
Engage			
Explore			
Explain			
Apply			
Share			
Reflect			
Extend			

FIGURE 7.1 Student-Centered Planning

So let's reconsider a couple of the case studies and what the learning experiences described in them might look like if implemented in a distance learning situation. I'm first drawn to reconsider Drew's work with his ninth graders and the constraint he imposed: no stand-and-deliver presentations. Those students, before there was a notion of a school shutdown, were already independently exploring content, collaborating with each other, researching, interacting with Drew for direct instruction, and making determinations for themselves about how to best demonstrate their skills and convey their learning with depth. The digital tools they found, learned, and incorporated into their projects were well suited for synchronous and asynchronous distance learning with any type of device.

Particularly challenging during the shutdown was the continued examination of literature. My email and social media feeds were flooded with requests from teachers for guidance in finding class sets of novels for their students to read. In some cases, such as the Gatsby example I consider in this book, the text is available online as a Gutenberg electronic text so students could still read the novel and make use of assistive browser extensions to hear it as an audio text. We were fortunate that many organizations that kept the bulk of their resources and materials provided them for free during the shutdown. Given that access to Gatsby wasn't a tremendous issue, the next question is how might we adapt the unit for distance learning? Returning to one of the teacher's goals (understanding the impact of Nick's unreliability as a narrator on the story) and the various questions the students used to frame their reading of the novel, we can find rich distance learning opportunities. Students could work as groups based on a common design question. For example, let's use: How might we question assumptions (Who says he is unreliable?). Students could read as partners, annotating a shared digital text. When student A finds a passage that prompts her to question Nick's reliability, she highlights it and explains what questions she is prompted to ask. Partner B does the same as he reads. Then, the partners reread and reply to each other's annotations. In essence, they are having a dialogue about the text that is embedded in the text. Their document can be shared with the teacher who can monitor and contribute to the discussion. Remember those days in the in-person classroom when you would assign a reading to students and tell them that the next day they would be having a discussion about it? And come the next day you spent most of the discussion asking the students to reference the text when they made contributions? Well, now those students are primed for using the text, and you can have your discussion synchronously in a virtual class meeting or asynchronously on a platform like Flipgrid. You can share selections from the students' annotations on all different guiding questions as models and to give students windows into the different lenses through which their classmates are reading. Ultimately, students could use a variety of media to explain the answers they derived to their questions from TikTok videos to infographics to choose-your-own adventure stories, all of which can be shared with a wide audience beyond the class for consideration and feedback.

Whatever form school takes—in-person, distance, or blended—I encourage you to invest time and energy in the same reflective practices we recommend for our students and apply your design thinking mindset to your student-centered pedagogical practice as the educational landscape continues to shift under us. To that end, I offer these two organizers to help you collect your evidence, thoughts, and insights around what makes for effective student-centered learning in general and distance learning strategies in particular. Figure 7.2 uses educator-facing learning targets to prompt reflection on the choices made during unit design and implementation, and Figure 7.3 turns those learning targets into a single-point rubric that can be used for both review and future goal-setting. Both can easily be adapted for students to use by replacing the teacher-facing learning targets with the student learning targets for your units.

Evidence and Reflection

Learning Target	Evidence	Insight
I can design distance learning units that promote connection, collaboration, and critical thinking.	I created...	Now I realize...
I can utilize platforms that engage students and allow for deep learning, interactivity and reflection.	I chose...	So going forward...
I can step out of my comfort zone with confidence.	I tried...	Because of that...

FIGURE 7.2 Evidence and Reflection

Single-Point Rubric

Areas for Growth	Learning Target	Points of Success
	I design distance learning units that promote connection, collaboration, and critical thinking.	
	I utilize platforms that engage students and allow for deep learning, interactivity and reflection.	
	I step out of my comfort zone with confidence.	

FIGURE 7.3 Single-Point Rubric

Notes

You can't properly interpret what's going on unless you first properly understand what's going on. And you can't properly apply your learning unless you have a good interpretation.

8

Conclusions: Mindset Matters Most

Given that I have presented you with a design thinking model (see Figure 3.1) and that a quick web search will return models by leading experts in design including IDEO, d.school, and Future Design School, it is easy to think of design as a process. It is useful to have these models to follow as you practice the different elements of design. Ultimately, I hope that you see design as a mindset rather than a process. In doing so, human-centered design can not only coexist with the other theories, practices, and methodologies of your learning space, but it can enhance them. When a design thinking mindset is applied to existing protocols a human-centered culture emerges. Consider the persona of Mitch, the school counselor. At this point you are adept at understanding a stakeholder. Notice how Mitch is seeking trusting, collaborative relationships with his colleagues. By infusing human-centered design into standard parts of a day in the life of your school—PPTs and 504 meetings; faculty meetings; curriculum writing and lesson planning; crisis intervention and task forces—you begin changing culture in a way that validates everyone's experiences, amplifies the voices of all learning community members, and builds collaborative relationships with open channels for dialogue and feedback. In this kind of culture, Mitch (and his fellow counselors) would find allies in the classroom teachers and other faculty—all working to address student mental health and future readiness.

This book could not be written without the ideas and feedback of so many people because human-centered design is collaborative by nature. It is written in the first person because the process is personal, individualized, and responsive to the needs, interests, and talents of everyone involved. The case studies presented here demonstrate a range of ways that teachers are embracing design thinking as pedagogy and the ways in which that practice is transforming their relationships with their students and their colleagues. Whether you work with high school students like Meredith, Drew, and Michelle or primary grade students like Arianna, design is not just something that you can do: it is a mindset your students can adopt. And when they do, their motivation for engaging in learning shifts. Arianna is witnessing her students let go of extrinsic motivators like grades as the inherent value and relevance of what they are learning takes over and motivates their engagement. And, whether you teach in a well-resourced community like Ashley or at a school in an area with high rates of poverty like Rachel, design is an optimistic, problem-solving orientation that is accessible to all educators and all students. I hope that in each of those real stories you find educators and students who are familiar or issues and concerns that resonate with you at your school. I hope that you take kernels of ideas from the process that these educators have used to take steps on your path, wherever you are on it, to transform your classroom, library, or school to be a future-focused, problem-solving space full of innovative possibilities. And student centered by design.

By using the personas to practice applying design thinking to problem solving, we keep stakeholders at the center of the process. I was taught a few key mindset tenets when studying with Future Design School. The first is that empathy is at the core of everything. That is why the personas are so important to how you explore this process. Keeping those people in mind throughout research and ideation encourages you to broaden your thinking beyond what you know, what is familiar to you, and how you experience a situation, and expand to embrace someone else's point of view, experiences, needs, and talents. When you think back on the personas now, were you particularly challenged by any of them? Was it difficult to identify what someone thought, did, said, or felt? Or, once you practiced, did you find that you were struck by aspects of a person that began to resonate with you and make you wonder about a student or colleague at your school and what elements of their background you might have overlooked and will now consider? When you apply a design thinking mindset to curriculum writing and lesson planning you stop designing for standards and instead design for students, with standards in mind. Maybe the problem you are facing is that some students aren't meeting certain standards. Or maybe new standards are a constraint within which you must revise curriculum. Either way, you are designing for the students, so keeping what they think, say, feel, do, and need at the center of your process is essential.

Another tenet taught by Future Design School that informs the processes explored in this book is that we must fall in love with the problem with which we are faced and not the first solutions that come to mind. The more openly we embrace the problem, live in it, and understand its nuance, the more the solutions we discover will be effective, iterative, and long-lasting. Even though Jen De Lisi-Hall lives her problem as a parent and as an educator, she extended her empathy network by interviewing and seeking the feedback of many other educators working to meet the needs of the wide range of learners in their classrooms and many parents trying to support their neurodiverse children and understand their individual learning plans. Because Jen spent so much time interacting with these different stakeholders, she was able to see when she needed to shift focus from a teacher-facing app to a family-facing one. In a design process it is important to give yourself permission to pivot, change course, and rethink where you are going. If you are committed to your solution and aloof from the problem, this is almost impossible to do.

If you fall in love with the problem, you then become able to see challenges as opportunities. Remember Rachel and her students who reported incidents of bullying in her classroom? Certainly, what she experienced is happening in schools just about everywhere. And the problem her students presented became the opportunity for them to gain agency as the designers of the solution. They researched the problem, they thought divergently in the ideation phase, and collaborated when their thinking converged during the creation phase. And, in this context, consider my challenge: under enrollment at my workshops. That challenge could have pushed me in several directions: cancel the workshops or revert to more traditional content. Heck, I could have said, "This isn't working; I'm going back to teaching." Instead, the challenge became an opportunity to be entrepreneurial. Rather than dial back on what I was doing, I leaned into it. I could see the possibility that the problem wasn't that I was being too innovative; it was that I wasn't being innovative enough.

Using a human-centered design approach to decision making opens us up to so many rich and varied possibilities. The process is not so much a formula as a mindset, and it inspires optimism. Using a "How might we . . ." question and fourth power word keeps us focused on possibilities and the value of collaborative work. Consider the ways in which the HMW questions used by the teachers and classes in each of the case studies kept the focus of the design on the students as the primary stakeholders:

> *How might we empower kids to self-advocate for their learning needs?*
> *How might we disrupt the traditional classroom structure to empower students to be agents of change and to take informed action?*
> *How might we disrupt senioritis?*
> *How might we leverage found time to amplify student-directed learning?*
> *How might we coax students to struggle?*
> *How might we eliminate bullying in our classroom?*

Notice how wide-ranging and far-reaching the subjects of these questions are. Design cycles are like snowflakes: no two are ever exactly alike. The process can't get stale; instead it is endlessly invigorating. Participants learn something new about themselves, each other, and their stakeholders every time they apply human-centered design to problem solving.

So many of us describe ourselves as being "not creative." Nothing can be further from the truth. We are born creative, wondering, tinkers. Babies and toddlers learn by trying, failing, and trying again. When given crayons and paper, what toddler says that their drawing isn't any good? None that I have met. And then something changes. For some reason, many of us stop flexing our creativity muscles, and, like any unused muscle, they atrophy. If we commit to flexing those muscles everyday, they will tone, lengthen, and strengthen. Like learning a language or a sport or an instrument, creative capacity grows with practice and training.

Creativity is, dare I say, educated out of us. Frankly, saying so doesn't require any daring. Sir Ken Robinson asserted in 2006 that schools kill creativity in his TED Talk of the same name, and his argument is quite convincing. His talk has over sixty-four million views. Design is the antidote. Human-centered design requires what Tom and David Kelley (@kelleybros on Twitter) call "creative confidence." In fact, that is the title of their acclaimed book about unleashing your creative potential. When you think of someone that you might describe as a creative genius, who comes to mind? Maya Angelou? Mozart? Lady Gaga? Ai Weiwei? Frida Kahlo? When referencing the work of Professor Dean Keith Simonton of the University of California, Davis, the Kelley brothers assert that these geniuses experienced prolific failures. It was their willingness to, as the Kelley brothers say, "take more shots at the goal" that sets them apart from the rest of us (p. 40). The beauty of design is that it nurtures creative confidence in those who engage in it. The process of divergent thinking coaxes us to let go of constraints, limitations, and judgment and let our imaginations explore possibilities.

In this way, there are so many lessons and tools to take from improvisational theater; certainly improv actors whose craft requires quick and divergent thinking on their feet in response to the cues of fellow actors exude creative confidence. When we practice the seminal improv technique, "Yes, And . . ." we see that none of us have all the best and most creative ideas. The best and most creative ideas come from us, together. The saying may be trite, still, design proves it to be true: the smartest (best, most creative, etc.) person in the room is the room. We all have rooms. We can all be designers. Let's engage in ongoing sharing of what we are doing.

Follow the educators whose stories you have read, and when you share on social media about the innovative teaching and learning in which you are engaged, use #SCLbydesign so we can follow each other's journeys.

Thank you!

Jacquelyn Whiting
@MsJWhiting (Twitter)
@jacqueylnwhiting (Instagram)

Appendix A: Resources

Abstract: The Art of Design
    bit.ly/AbstractNetDoc

Dove's ad about beauty standards and young girls
    bit.ly/Dovebeauty

Google Trend's "Year in Search" videos
    bit.ly/Yis2019

Google's Applied Digital Skills
    bit.ly/ADSgoogle

Greenpeace's response to Dove
    bit.ly/gpresponse

"How might we . . ." question template
    bit.ly/HMWCopy

Interpretation phase organizer
    bit.ly/ProbAssetQ

SHEG teaching resources
    cor.stanford.edu

"The Sift" newsletter from the *News Literacy Project*
    bit.ly/NLPSift

Stanford History Education Group (SHEG) report on civic online reasoning
    bit.ly/SHEGreport

Solve in Time
    https://solveintime.com

Student-Centered Planning
    bit.ly/SCplanning

Understanding your stakeholder organizer
    bit.ly/SHorganizer

Universal Declaration of Human Rights
    un.org/en/universal-declaration-human-rights

Appendix B: Templates and Organizers

As a quick reference, or in case you've already used the templates and organizers that fall in the chapters, I have provided a clean copy of each for you to reuse here.

Design Process

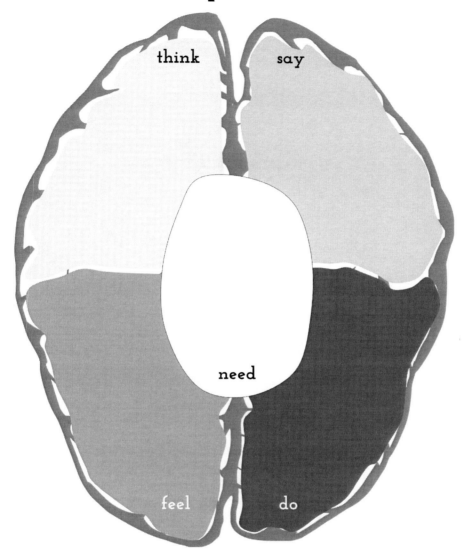

Understand Your Stakeholder

Problem Statement

(<u>stakeholder</u>) needs (<u>unmet need</u>) because (<u>insight/asset</u>).

_____ needs _____ because _____
(stakeholder)

_____

Resources & Insights

_____ likes…
(stakeholder)

_____ knows s/he/they is good at…
(stakeholder)

_____ wishes…
(stakeholder)

Build a Draft Question

How might we _____ in order to _____ ?

How might we… ?

How might we… ?

How might we… ?

Problem Template

How might we _____ (the 4th word)

_____ (insight, resource, motivation, etc.)

to help _____ (describe the stakeholder)

who need _____ (unmet need)

to _____ (goal)

HMW Template

How might we ... (the 4th word)

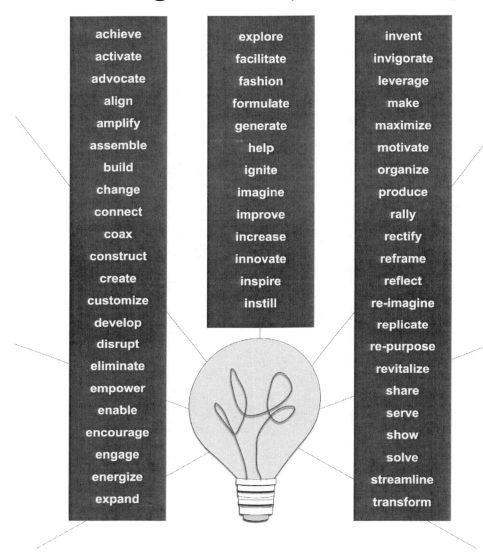

achieve	explore	invent
activate	facilitate	invigorate
advocate	fashion	leverage
align	formulate	make
amplify	generate	maximize
assemble	help	motivate
build	ignite	organize
change	imagine	produce
connect	improve	rally
coax	increase	rectify
construct	innovate	reframe
create	inspire	reflect
customize	instill	re-imagine
develop		replicate
disrupt		re-purpose
eliminate		revitalize
empower		share
enable		serve
encourage		show
engage		solve
energize		streamline
expand		transform

The Fourth Word

Digging into the Problem

What is the problem?

Who is affected by this problem?
How many people? How old are they? What are their current behaviors? Where do they live? Who might be impacted by the potential solutions?

When did this problem start and what might happen if nothing is done about it?

Why does this problem concern you? Why should other people be concerned about this problem?

Source Citations

Digging into the Problem Organizer

	Before Unit Implementation		Upon Unit Completion
	What will the students do? (curiosity, agency, risk-taking, collaboration)	How will I know it worked? (gather formative and summative evidence)	Did it work? (what modifications are necessary?)
Engage			
Explore			
Explain			
Apply			
Share			
Reflect			
Extend			

Student-Centered Planning

Appendix C: Technology Resources

Design, as a process, is not dependent on technology or technology driven. Furthermore, just as Moore's law describes the exponential increase in computing power, the pace of iteration and evolution of educational technology is astounding at best and even overwhelming. That pace of change, coupled with protecting data privacy, and the fluid pricing structures of educational technology make it difficult to recommend particular platforms. That being said, at this moment, here are some of my preferred platforms that can support your design work. Rest assured, these tools and platforms will evolve. Some will disappear. New ones will replace and improve on them. As you find useful tools for your design work, share them with #SCLbydesign for everyone to try.

Adobe Spark
spark.adobe.com
> Adobe Spark couldn't make the creation of posters, slide shows, and videos any easier. It is a drag-and-drop platform that enables the creation of professional-looking visual materials.

Glide App
glideapps.com
> Glide App makes app prototyping so easy to plan, to design, to build, as well as to edit and revise. Add your info—including images—to a Google Sheet, and presto, you have an app!

Google Docs
docs.google.com
> Google Docs are an easy-to-use tool for collaboration. The comment feature combined with the ability to assign tasks to people streamlines task management.

Google Slides and Google Draw

Google Slides and Google Draw are the unsung heroes of the Gsuite tools. Both enable synchronous collaboration like Google Docs. Either can be used to create visually potent and arresting promotional materials as well as serve as curation and brainstorming platforms.

Jamboard
jamboard.google.com

Jamboard is Google's digital, collaborative white board. There is a web-based version and an app. On a touchscreen device (chromebook, smartphone, or tablet) you can use the app which is the more powerful version, complete with sync to the materials in your Google Drive and assistive technology that includes shape and text recognition.

KialoEdu
kialo-edu.com

KialoEdu, like Parlay, is a platform where design teams can map and discuss ideas, posting pro- and con- arguments, evidence, and sources.

Padlet
padlet.com

Padlet is a collaborative, digital bulletin board. Your team could use Padlet to collect and organize ideas and resources including text, images, and video.

Parlay
parlayideas.com

Parlay, like KialoEdu, is a platform where design teams can map and discuss ideas, posting pro- and con- arguments, evidence, and sources.

Wakelet
wakelet.com

Wakelet is a platform you can use to organize and share information about your team's focus problem, research, brainstorming, etc. You can collect and organize all sorts of multimedia resources for collaboration.

References

Cohen, Michael. *Educated by Design*. San Diego: Dave Burgess Consulting, 2018.

Devers, Amy, and Jaime Derringer. *Clever*, 2019. Episode 82: David Schwarz of HUSH Studios. Podcast. Available at https://www.listennotes.com/podcasts/clever/ep-82-david-schwarz-of-hush—K7v41PxTBk.

The Field Guide to Human-Centered Design. 2015. IDEO.org. Available at https://www.designkit.org/human-centered-design.

"Ilse Crawford: Interior Design." *Abstract: The Art of Design*, 2017. Season 1, Episode 8. Netflix Series.

Jacob, Brian A. 2017. *What We Know about Career and Technical Education in High School*. Available at brookings.edu/research/what-we-know-about-career-and-technical-education-in-high-school. Accessed January 5, 2020.

Kelley, Tom, and David Kelley. *Creative Confidence: Unleashing the Creative Potential within Us All*. New York: Currency, 2013.

Leonard, Kelly, and Tom Yorton. *Yes, And: How Improvisation Reverses "No, But" Thinking and Improves Creativity and Collaboration—Lessons from The Second City*. New York: Harper Business, 2015.

Maeda, John. *How to Speak Machine*. New York: Penguin, 2019.

Pixar in a Box: The Art of Storytelling. Khan Academy. Available at https://www.khanacademy.org/partner-content/pixar/storytelling.

Robinson, Ken. *Do Schools Kill Creativity?* TED, 2006. Available at https://www.ted.com/talks/sir_ken_robinson_do_schools_kill_creativity. Accessed February 15, 2020.

Index

Note: Page numbers in italics indicate figures.

Abstract: The Art of Design, 2–3, 35, 111
Accommodations, 90–92
Activism, 11–12
   activist student persona (Adrian), 11–12, 58
   civics class public policy paper, 83–85
   global perspective (Afghan girl), 73–78, *75–77*
   social media, 58–63
Adobe Spark, 45, 121
Adrian (activist student persona), 11–12, 58
Advanced placement (AP) chemistry, 12, 64–67, *65–67*
   "found time," using, 36, 64, *65*
   HMW question, 36, *65*
   Honors Chem class and, 36, 64, *65–66*
Afghanistan (Parvana case study), 73–78, *75–77*
Antonella (fifth grader persona), 12, 73, *80*
AP chemistry. *See* Advanced placement chemistry
Arianna (elementary teacher), 76–77, 107–108
Ashley (CTE teacher), 81–82
At-home activities, 95
Athletic director persona, 10

Benjamin (student persona), 10–11, *23*, 52
"Brain" organizer, 21, *22–23*
   librarian (Lois), *57*
   students, *23*, *79*, *80*
   teacher (Julie), *38–39*
   understand your stakeholder, 21, *22*, 112, *115*
Brainstorming, 41–45
   Crazy 8s, 41, *42–44*, *66*
   group brainstorm, 61–62, *61*
   How ideas, 45
   Wow! ideas, 45
   "Yes! And . . ." technique, 45, 64
   See also Case studies
Breadwinner (Ellis), 73
Building administrator persona (Gloria), 10, 40, 89
Bullying (case study), 88–89, 109

Career and technical education (CTE), 81–82
Case studies, 51–96
   advanced placement chemistry, 64–67, *65–67*
   bullying, eliminating, 88–89, 109
   career and technical education (CTE), 81–82

Case studies (*cont.*)
  civics class public policy paper, 83–85
  digital literacy class, 58–63
  game-based design, 93–96
  Great Gatsby essay, 68–69, 102
  multigrade classroom, 86–87
  promoting student agency, 90–92
  safe learning environment (third grade), 88–89
  social studies (sixth grade), 73–78, *79–80*
  sociology class (high school), 52–57
  Solve in Time, 93–96
  special education programs, 90–92
  TurnSignal app, 90–92, *92*
  world history (ninth grade), 70–72
Chemistry class. *See* Advanced placement chemistry
Cheryl (midcareer teacher), 7–8, 35
Civics class, 83–85
Clever (podcast), 32–33
Cohen, Michael, 3, 54
Colati, Drew, 70–72, 102
Collaboration, 15–16, 35–50, 56, 107
  Crazy 8s peer collaboration, 41, *42–44*, *66*
  culture of, 8–9
  design exercises and, 54
  HMW questions, 36, 40
  insights, 40
  intersections of needs/insights, 40–41
  problem statement, 40
  teacher-student ratio and, 56
  unpacking a teacher persona, 36–41, *38–39*
  "Yes! And . . ." technique, 45, 64
  See also Case studies
Colleagues, 35–50
  collegial intersections of needs/insights, 40–41
  See also Collaboration; Personas
Cottier, Emma, 73–78
Counselor (school counselor persona), 9
COVID pandemic and shutdowns, 99–103
Crawford, Ilse, 35–36
Crazy 8s, 41, *42–44*, *66*
Creativity, *17*, 31, 109–110
  feedback and, 33
  HMW questions for, 27, *28–30*
CTE (career and technical education), 81–82

Curricula
  content standards, 19
  Design Thinking for High School Students, 53
  evolution of, 24
  Moore's law and, 24
  prototypes, 32
Curriculum design, 19–34
  (1) identifying a problem/goal, 20
  (2) developing empathy with stakeholders, 20–24
  (3) constraints and interpretations, 24–31
  (4) prototype, feedback, and testing, 31–33, 45–49
  collaboration in, 35–50
  HMW questions and, 27–31, *28–30*
  as opportunity to reexamine, 20
  team process in, 20, 27–31

Darren (new teacher), 8, 40
De Lisi-Hall, Jennifer (Jen), 90–92, 108
Dee (Solve in Time case study), 93–96
Design, 1–5, 15–17
  creativity and, 109–110
  of curricula, 19–34
  mindset for, 107–110
  as team process, 15–16, 20
  See also Case studies; Design process; Human-centered design
Design examples. *See* Case studies
Design of curricula. *See* Curriculum design
Design process, 1–5, 15–17, *114*
  collaboration in, 35–50
  collaborative team and, 15–16
  empathy in, 15, *17*
  identifying a problem, 20
  inquiry in, 15, *17*
  as iterative, 3, 15, *17*, 49, 54–55, 108
  map of, *17*, *114*
  possibilities in, 15, *17*
  steps in, 20–33
Design sprint, 53–54
Design thinking, 3–4, 53
Design Thinking for Educators, 94
Devers, Amy, 33
Digital literacy class, 58–63
Distance learning, 99–105
Divergent thinking, 31, 109

Diversity, 9, 90–92
Drew (social studies teacher), 70–72, 102

Emma (social studies teacher), 73–78
Empathy, 2, 15, 36
  in case studies, 54, 59, 73–74, 87
  in map of design process, *17*
  with stakeholders, 20–24
Empowerment, 19–34, 35–50, 51, 55, 90–92
English class (case study), 68–69
Entrepreneurial educator (Jen/ TurnSignal app), 90–92, 108
Evidence and reflection, *104*

Faculty personas. *See* Teacher/faculty personas
Feedback, 31–33, 93
  on prototypes, 49
"Five Whys" protocol, 84
Found time, using, 36, 64, *65*
Fourth Word, *29*, 109, *118*
Future Design School, 24, 53, 108

Game-based design, 93–96
Gay-Straight Alliance (GSA), 11
Gender identity, 52–53
GlideApp, 121
Gloria (administrator/assistant principal), 10, 35, 40, 89
Google, 71, 121–122
  Applied Digital Skills, 58, 111
  Google Docs, 121
  Google Draw, 78, 122
  Google Maps, 87
  Google Slides, 122
  "Year in Search" videos, 55, 111
Google Certified Trainers and Innovators, 53, 73
Google Innovator Academy, 90, 94
Great Gatsby essay, 68–69, 102
Greenpeace, 53, 111
Gutenberg electronic text, 102

Hero's journey, 47, *48*
High school sociology class, 52–57
HMW. *See* How might we . . . ? (HMW)
"How" ideas, 45
How might we . . . ? (HMW), 27–31, 36, 109
  The Fourth Word, *29*, 109, *118*
  HMW question (on problem template), *25–26*
  HMW questions in case studies, 36, 59, 64
  template for, *28–30*, *117*
Human rights, 73–78
Human-centered design, 1–5, 35–50
  brainstorming, 41, *42–44*, 55
  empathy in, 2–3
  examples (case studies), 51–96
  ideation, 41
  mindset and, 107–110
  prototyping, 45–49, *46–48*
  unpacking a teacher persona, 36–41, *38–39*
  See also Case studies

Ideation, creative, *17*, 31
  feedback and, 33
  HMW questions and, 27, *28–30*
Individualized education programs (IEPs), 90–92
Industrial arts. *See* Career and technical education (CTE)
Inquiry, 15
Interpretation phase, 24–31, 111
Iteration, 3, 15, *17*, 49, 54–55, 108

Jacobs, Brian A., 81
Jamboard, 122
Jay (sixth grader persona), 12, 73, *79*
Jen (entrepreneurial educator), 90–92, 108
Jocelyn (third grader persona), 13
Julie (veteran teacher), 8, 35, 36–41, *38–39*
  HMW question for, 40
  unpacking teacher persona, 36–41, *38–39*

Kai (teacher new to this school), 8, 35, 40
Kelley, Tom and David, 110
KialoEdu, 122

Lambert, Arianna, 76–77, 107–108
Lanier, Dee, 93–96
Learning environment, safe, 88–89
Learning modalities, 70–72, 102
Learning targets, 103, *104–105*
LGBTQ students, 11–12

Library learning commons persona (Lois), 9, 55–56, *57*
Lois (library learning commons), 9, 55–56, *57*

Maher, Michelle, 52–55
Make Just One Change (Rothstein and Santana), 52
Meredith (civics class teacher), 83–84
Michelle (social studies teacher), 52–55
Mindset, 107–110
   for curriculum development, 19–34
   problem-solving, 86–87
Minimum viable product (MVP), 32, 91
Mitch (school counselor), 9, 89, 107
Moore, Gordon, 24, 49
Moore's law, 24, 49, 121
Multigrade classroom, 86–87
MVP (minimum viable product), 32, 91

Naomi (student persona), 11
Needs. *See* "Brain" organizer
News Literacy Project, 58, 112

O'Connor, Ashley, 81–82
Organizers. *See* Templates and organizers

Padlet, 62, 122
Pandemic and shutdowns, 99–103
Parlay, 122
Parvana (Afghan girl), 73–78, *75–77*
Personas, 7–14
   other staff, 9–10
   students, 10–13
   teachers, 7–9
   See also Student personas; Teacher/faculty personas
Planning and Placement Team (PPT) process, 91
Problem
   identifying, 20
   loving, 24, 108–109
   statement, *25–26*
   template, *25–26, 116*
Problem solving, 108–109
   in CTE classes, 82
   Digging into the Problem Organizer, 84, *85, 119*
   in a multigrade classroom, 86–87
   real-world, with game-based design, 93–96
   Solve in Time, 93–96, 112

Prototypes, 31–33, 45–49, *46–48*
   in case studies, 54, 62–63
   curriculum prototypes, 32
   feedback on, 49
   goal of, 47
   hero's journey, 47, *48*
   importance and use of, 32, 45
   storyboard, 46, *47*
   types of, 32, 45–47
Public policy paper (case study), 83–85

Q-focus, 52–53
QFT protocol, 52–53
Question: How might we . . . ?. *See* How might we . . . ? (HMW)

Rachel (bullying case study), 88–89, 108, 109
Ramsey, Meredith, 83–84
Real-world research, 55–56, *57*
Resources, 111–122
Right Question Institute, 52–53
Robinson, Sir Ken, 109

Safe learning environment (3rd grade), 88–89
School counselor persona (Mitch), 9, 89, 107
Schools
   culture of collaboration, 8–9
   support staff personas, 10
Schwartz, David, 33
Senioritis, 52–56
SHEG (Stanford History Education Group), 58, 111
"The Sift" (newsletter), 58, 112
Single-point rubric, *105*
SmashboardEDU, 94
Social media, 3–4, 58–63
   defining, 58
   HMW question, 59, *60*
   pros and cons, 58–59
   specific tags in, 3, 4
Social studies class, 73–78, *79–80*
Sociology class, 52–57
Solve in Time, 93–96, 112
Special education programs, 90–92
Stakeholders, 1–2, 3, 20–31, 108–109
   developing empathy with, 20–24, 36
   multiple, 31
   students as, 20–21, 109
   teacher as, *38–39*

understanding ("brain" organizer), 21, 22–23, 38–39, 73, 112, 115
Standards
  as an asset, 31
  in curriculum design, 19
  on HMW template, 30
Stanford History Education Group (SHEG), 58, 111
Stanley (athletic director), 10, 35
STEM, 81, 93
Storyboard prototype, 46, 47
Student agency (case study), 90–92
Student-Centered Planning template, 100, 101, 112, 120
Student-directed learning (case study), 64–67
Student personas, 10–13
  Adrian (budding activist), 11–12, 58
  Antonella (fifth grader), 12, 73, 80
  Benjamin (content with average), 10–11, 23, 52
  Jay (sixth grader), 12, 73, 79
  Jocelyn (third grader), 13
  Naomi (presentation vs. reality), 11
Students
  accommodations for, 90–92
  as agents of change, 51–96
  buy-in of, 53–54
  design sprint, 53–54
  as design thinkers, 51–96
  empowering, 19–34, 35–50, 51–96
  enhancing learning through collaboration, 35–50
  learning modalities for, 70–72, 102
  as stakeholders in curriculum design, 20–21, 109
  See also Case studies
Support staff personas, 9–10
Swanson, Rachel, 88–89, 108, 109

Teacher/faculty personas, 7–9, 35–41
  Cheryl (midcareer teacher), 7–8, 35
  Darren (new teacher), 8, 40
  Gloria (building administrator), 10, 35, 40, 89
  Julie (veteran teacher), 8, 35, 36–41, 38–39
  Kai (teacher new to this school), 8, 35, 40
  Lois (library learning commons), 9, 55–56, 57
  Mitch (school counselor), 9, 89, 107
  Stanley (athletic director), 10, 35
  unpacking, 36–41, 38–39
  See also Student personas
Teacher-student ratio, 56
Teachers
  as designers, 3
  needs of, 39, 40
  organizers, 103, 104–105
  personas of, 7–9, 35–41
  See also Case studies
Teacher-student ratio, 56
Team process, 15–16, 20, 35–36
  HMW questions and, 27–31
  multiple stakeholders to inform, 31
  See also Collaboration
Technology resources, 121–122
TechRabbi (Michael Cohen), 3
Templates and organizers, 103, 113–120
  "Brain" organizer (Understand Your Stakeholder), 21, 22, 112, 115
  Design Process, 17, 114
  Digging into the Problem Organizer, 84, 85, 119
  Evidence and Reflection, 104
  "The Fourth Word," 29, 118
  How might we . . . ? (HMW), 28–30, 117
  Problem Template, 25, 116
  Single-Point Rubric, 105
  Student-Centered Planning, 100, 101, 112, 120
Testing design ideas/prototypes, 31–33
TikTok, 71, 102
TurnSignal app, 90, 91–92, 92

Universal Declaration of Human Rights, 74, 112
Universal Design for Learning (UDL), 52, 100
Unpacking a teacher persona, 36–41, 38–39

Virtual classes (distance learning), 99–105

Wakelet, 122
Why
  "Five Whys" protocol, 84
  "Why" questions, 84
World history class, 70–72
Wow! ideas, 45

"Year in Search" videos, 55, 111
"Yes! And . . ." technique, 45, 64

About the Author

JACQUELYN WHITING is the innovation and technology specialist for Cooperative Educational Services (C.E.S.) in Trumbull, Connecticut. She has a bachelor's in government studies and studio art from Connecticut College and a master's in social studies and education from Southern Connecticut State University. She is also a Google Certified Innovator and has trained with Future Design School (Toronto). Jacquelyn is the coauthor of *News Literacy: The Keys to Combating Fake News* and has been published by EdSurge and other education forums. She presents frequently on human-centered design, student and educator voice, and innovative educational technology practices. You can follow her tweeting @MsJWhiting.

Made in United States
North Haven, CT
17 October 2023

42847533R00085